3500/1

C0-BVA-802

# MILITARY HELICOPTER DESIGN TECHNOLOGY

To the memory of Jenny

# MILITARY HELICOPTER DESIGN TECHNOLOGY

## Raymond W Prouty

JANE'S DEFENCE DATA

© Copyright Raymond W Prouty 1989
Artwork on pages 30, 31, 56, 76, 94, 109
© Copyright Jane's Information Group Limited 1989

Published in the United Kingdom in 1989 by Jane's
Defence Data, a division of Jane's Information
Group Limited, 'Jane's' is a registered trade mark.

Jane's Information Group Limited
163 Brighton Road
Coulsdon
Surrey CR3 2NX United Kingdom

ISBN 0 7106 0542 0

Distributed in the Philippines and the USA and its
dependencies by Jane's Information Group Inc.
1340 Braddock Place, Suite 300, PO Box 1436
Alexandria, Virginia 22313–2036

All rights are reserved. No part of this publication
may be reproduced, stored in a retrieval system,
transmitted in any form by any means electrical,
mechanical or photocopied, recorded or otherwise
without prior permission of the publisher.

Computer Typesetting by Columns of Reading

Printed and bound in the United Kingdom by Biddles Limited
Guildford and King's Lynn

# Contents

# Acknowledgements

Some of the material in this book, including both text and figures, first appeared in the 'Aerodynamics' column of *Rotor and Wing International* magazine. I am grateful for the kind permission to use it here.

I also want to thank Chuck Landers of McDonnell Douglas Helicopters Corporation for his helpful and constructive criticism of the manuscript and to both Chuck and Rob Mack, also of MDHC, for their cooperation in providing material on the Apache.

# Foreword

The design of any vehicle is an exercise in compromise, but this is probably more true in the case of a helicopter than of any other vehicle. In almost every decision, the designer must keep in mind that what is good for hover performance is bad for forward flight and what is good for forward flight is bad for hover. In no other vehicle will the relationship between empty weight and payload be so uncompromisingly one-to-one. In addition, the maximum speed limit of a 'pure' helicopter is apparently even more rigorously enforced by basic physical principles than was the 'sound barrier' that airplanes once faced. For these reasons, the helicopter designer cannot be said to be seeking the optimum design, but the 'least worse compromise'.

This book is intended to describe how the designer goes about this difficult task of creating not only a helicopter, but a helicopter system – especially as it is to be used by the military. The description is primarily based on what has actually been done over the past five decades with discussions of both successes and failures, and for this I have to thank the people in the helicopter industry for their willingness to share experiences of both types in written works and in conversations.

What is said about serious gardeners is probably true about helicopter designers – their natural state is one of continuous frustration, but they like to talk.

# EH Industries EH 101 (Basic Naval Version) Cutaway Drawing Key

1 Fixed horizontal tailplane
2 Tailplane construction
3 Pylon fin section, cambered to port
4 Tail rotor pylon, canted to port
5 Tail navigation light
6 Anti-collision light
7 Pylon tip fairing
8 Tail rotor hydraulic actuator
9 Final drive right-angle gearbox
10 Blade pitch change mechanism
11 Four-bladed tail rotor
12 All-composite tail rotor blades
13 Tail rotor drive shaft
14 Port tailplane segment
15 Bevel drive gearbox
16 All-composite pylon construction
17 Tailplane spar attachment joints
18 Main rotor blade high speed tip profile
19 Blade balance and tracking weight pockets
20 Folding tail pylon hinge joints
21 Tail rotor control rod
22 Transmission shaft coupling
23 Dorsal spine fairing
24 Tail rotor transmission shaft
25 Shaft bearings
26 Rear fuselage frame and stringer construction
27 Internal maintenance walkway
28 Aluminium alloy skin panelling
29 BAe Sea Skua anti-surface-vessel missile
30 BAe Sea Eagle anti-surface-vessel missile
31 Main undercarriage sponson tail fairing
32 Maintenance step
33 Engine air-start connection
34 Rear fuselage joint frame
35 Main undercarriage sponson composite construction
36 Mainwheel bay
37 Aft emergency flotation bag
38 Plessey HISOS dipping sonar
39 Marine markers
40 Mk 11 depth charge
41 Sonobuoys
42 Starboard mainwheel
43 Main undercarriage leg strut
44 Tie-down ring
45 Leg strut pivot fixing
46 Hydraulic retraction jack
47 Main undercarriage mounting support structure

48 Rear underfloor fuel tank
49 Honeycomb floor panel construction
50 Undercarriage mounting machined main frames
51 Pull-out cabin window panel
52 Tie down ring
53 Main cabin rear bulkhead
54 Maintenance walkway
55 Starboard engine exhaust duct
56 Auxiliary Power Unit (APU)
57 APU exhaust
58 Centre engine bay firewalls
59 Centre engine exhaust duct
60 Rearward sliding engine cowling box
61 Fire suppression bottles
62 Engine bay venting air intake
63 Centre (No 2) engine installation
64 Centre engine/gearbox drive shaft
65 APU intake
66 Starboard (No 3) engine bay
67 Intake particle separator by-pass duct
68 General Electric CT7-2A (T700-GE-401A) turboshaft engine
69 Engine accessory gearbox
70 Engine oil tank
71 Main engine mounting
72 Hinged engine cowling panels/work platforms
73 Rescue hoist/winch hinged mountings
74 Winch motor fairing
75 Engine washing connectors
76 Main cabin floor beam construction
77 Seat/equipment mounting rails
78 Pressure refuelling connection, gravity fillers on port side
79 Torpedo parachute launch packs
80 Door latch
81 Starboard emergency exit door
82 Fuel tank access panel
83 Main cabin floor panelling
84 Starboard engine air intake
85 Engine/gearbox drive shaft
86 Gearbox oil cooler
87 Rotor head hydraulic control jack (three)
88 Metal cored composite main rotor hub unit
89 Blade retention rings
90 Elastomeric blade root bearings
91 Rotor hub head fairing

92 Blade root bearing attachment fittings
93 Drag dampers
94 Blade folding hinge joints (deck stowage)
95 Blade root attachment fittings
96 Five-bladed main rotor
97 Swash plate mechanism
98 Port (No 1) engine intake fairing
99 Gearbox/rotor head fairing
100 Main reduction gearbox
101 Port engine/gearbox drive shaft
102 No 2 generator
103 Gearbox mounting struts
104 No 1 hydraulic system module
105 Bevel drive main gearbox input
106 Gearbox mounting sub-frame
107 Sliding door top rail
108 Sliding main cabin door
109 Forward underfloor fuel tanks
110 Marconi Stingray homing torpedos
111 Mk 46 lightweight torpedo
112 External stores carrier
113 Sliding door lower rail
114 GEC AQS-903 ASW mission avionics rack
115 Machined gearbox support main frame
116 CRT display screens
117 Maintenance walkway
118 Hydraulic system ground connections
119 Rotor brake
120 Accessory gearbox drive shaft
121 Airframe mounted accessory equipment gearbox
122 Forward sliding equipment bay cowling
123 No 1 and emergency generators
124 Nos 2 and 3 hydraulic system modules
125 Control rod linkages
126 Sliding cowling rail
127 ASW systems operator and Observer's seats
128 Forward cabin pull-out window panel
129 Double skinned lower fuselage hull construction
130 Battery
131 Ground power socket
132 Conditioned air distribution ducting
133 Starboard navigation light
134 Avionics equipment racks, port and starboard
135 Avionics cooling air exhaust duct
136 Automatic flight control system actuators (AFCS)

137 Port side crew entry door upper segment, open
138 Main rotor blade glassfibre skin panelling
139 Bonded heater mat
140 Leading-edge titanium erosion sheath
141 Composite steel/carbon-fibre main spar pockets
142 Glassfibre leading-edge spar
143 Honeycomb core trailing edge
144 Cockpit roof glazing
145 Control/equipment ducting forward fairing
146 Overhead engine condition-control levers
147 Cockpit rear bulkhead
148 Control rod linkages
149 Circuit breaker panel
150 Pilot's seat
151 Safety harness
152 Sliding, jettisonable side window panel
153 Window external emergency release handle
154 Cockpit section all-composite construction
155 Adjustable seat mounting rails
156 Cockpit floor level
157 Cockpit air distribution ducting
158 Static port
159 Electrical equipment bays
160 Ferranti Blue Kestrel 360-deg search radar
161 Ventral radome
162 Forward emergency flotation bag
163 Twin nosewheels, forward retracting
164 Nose undercarriage leg strut
165 Hydraulic steering jack
166 Nose undercarriage pivot fixing
167 Yaw control rudder pedals
168 Downward vision window
169 Cyclic pitch control column
170 Collective pitch control lever
171 Centre control console
172 CRT display instrument panel
173 Instrument panel shroud
174 Co-pilot's seat
175 Stand-by compass
176 Windsreen wipers
177 Curved windscreen panels, electrically heated
178 Composite nose section skin panelling
179 Hinged nose cone
180 Cockpit front bulkhead
181 Space provision for optional weather radar
182 Pitot heads (two)

# How We Got Where We Are

## Experiments and Dreams

Serious military interest in rotary wing aircraft goes all the way back to the First World War. To replace the vulnerable hydrogen-filled observation balloons, a trio of Hungarian engineers (including Theodore Von Karman) developed the PKZ-2, a three-engine tethered machine with counter-rotating propellers. Over 30 test flights were made before an accident and the Armistice put an end to the project.

The successful development and operation of fixed-wing aircraft during that war introduced

*The PKZ-2, developed by three Hungarian engineers in the First World War.*

the military not only to the capabilities of aeroplanes but to their limitations as well; specifically, their need for long runways and the necessity to keep moving to stay up and to maintain control. It was quite obvious that an aircraft not bound by these limitations could be effectively used in many military situations.

In 1921, some far-sighted members of the US Army Air Service were able to get a helicopter project started at McCook Field in Dayton, Ohio, just a few miles from the Wright Brothers' home. The project was directed by Dr George A. De Bothezat, a Russian émigré who in two years and with $2 million managed to put together a multi-rotor aircraft and to demonstrate its ability to slowly skitter a few feet above the

*The De Bothezat Helicopter built in Ohio (USA) in 1921, but abandoned in 1923.*

ground in approximately the direction the pilot desired.

Besides being aesthetically displeasing, it was over-weight and under-powered (a situation not entirely unknown to designers of modern helicopters). As a consequence, it never reached its guaranteed hover ceiling of 300 ft (91m), and in 1923 the project was abandoned.

Although it was not yet time for a military helicopter in the form of De Bothezat's con-

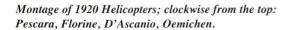

*Montage of 1920 Helicopters; clockwise from the top: Pescara, Florine, D'Ascanio, Oemichen.*

*Cierva's Autogiro demonstrated the military potential of rotary-wing aircraft.*

figuration, the military requirement remained recognised but unfullfilled.

During the 1920s, the military aviation thinkers in all nations kept abreast of the sporadic helicopter development. They observed with interest as marginally sucessfull one-shot projects briefly blossomed and then faded in France, England, Spain, Russia, Belgium and the USA. Flights of ten minutes and two miles set records in this era.

In the publicity that these helicopter projects received, the military potential of another rotary wing development was at first almost ignored. This was the autogiro as developed by Juan de la Cierva in Spain and successfully demonstrated in l923. Unlike the rotor on a helicopter, the rotor on Cierva's aircraft was not powered by the engine but was kept windmilling by the flow of air going through it from the underside as the aircraft was pulled along by its propeller.

From Cierva's point of view, the autogiro was simply an aeroplane that happened to have an unusual wing. The advantage of this unusual wing was that because it would rotate at quite low forward speeds, it reduced the effective stall speed from 50 kts (92.6 km/h) – common to aeroplanes of the day – to around 20 kts (about 45 km/h) with an accompanying reduction in the required length of runway.

The autogiro reached its full development in the late 1930s. It could then demonstrate operation out of and in to tennis-court-sized areas and fly at over 120 kts (222 km/h).

At this stage, the military aviators saw potential in the autogiro for roles associated with battlefield observation and liaison where a small area next to the headquarters tent could serve as an airfield. The US Army bought several from Cierva's US licensees for evaluation; first on the plains of Oklahoma and then as more uses

*The Kellet YO-60 was flown from aircraft carriers.*

suggested themselves, in the jungles of Central America and to and from aircraft carriers at sea. Similar evaluations of the autogiro were taking place in several of the other armies of the world as international tension mounted prior to the Second World War.

These tests showed that the autogiro had some useful characteristics but it was also evident that it would be even more useful if only it could hover.

The development of the aircraft that could hover, the helicopter, had not been entirely neglected. By the late 1930s, Focke and Flettner in Germany, Breguet in France, and Sikorsky in the USA had prototypes that could not only

*(clockwise): the Breguet counter-rotating prototype which flew in the 1930s; the Flettner Fl 265V1 featured an anti-torque trim surface on the rudder – the helicopter crashed when the intermeshing blades collided, and; Igor Sikorsky at the controls of the VS-300 in 1941, a year after his first free helicopter flight on 13 May 1940.*

hover but could make cross-country flights at speeds of 60 (111 km/h) to 80 kts (148 km/h).

Thus when war came, some autogiros were used by the armies of the major combatants, but at the same time, the demand was for the speedy development of the helicopter. With the fall of France, the Breguet effort was halted but designers in both Germany and in the USA were put under contract to produce in large numbers. Despite this encouragement, the actual development was too little and too late to have any significant effect on the war effort. Flettner in Germany was able to produce only 24 of his Fl 282s before Allied bombers destroyed his factory near Munich.

On the other side of Germany, in Berlin, Hitler had ordered Focke to build 400 a month of his Fa 223s but the Russians captured the underground factory after only nine had been rolled out. Of the 33 helicopters that did get into the German service, some Flettners were used for anti-submarine operations and some Fockes as support aircraft in the Alps.

Sikorsky in Connecticut also had problems but they had mainly to do with the low priority of

*The Flettner 282 made no effect on the Nazi war effort but demonstrated the ability of German industry in rotary-wing aviation.*

the helicopter with respect to strategic materials and skilled workers. Nevertheless, he rapidly developed three helicopters, the R-4, R-5, and R-6 and by VJ day had delivered more than 400 to the US Army, Navy, and Coast Guard and to the United Kingdom. A few served in the closing stages of the Pacific war but most got no further than various training and testing facilities.

*The Focke-Achgelis 223 was operational in southern Germany before Germany's surrender.*

*Igor Sikorsky's early designs: (above) the R-4B (US Navy designation HNS-1); the R-5/H-5 (later S-51) and (bottom right) the R-6 Hoverfly II.*

# Postwar Developments

Although coming too late to have a significant impact on the outcome of the Second World War, the helicopter clearly showed potential and it was accepted by all military establishments as a necessary part of their organisations. For this reason, the development continued, supported primarily by the military but with a few enthusiasts embarking on purely commercial endeavours that in several cases became the foundations for subsequent military programmes.

In America during the postwar years, continuing development resulted in the procurement of the Sikorsky S-5l as the H-5 for the Air Force and as the HO3S for the Navy and Coast Guard. The smaller Sikorsky S-52 was delivered to the Marines as the HO5S. The Bell factory in upstate New York was busy producing their Model 47 which was used as the H-13 and HTL-3 by the Army, Navy, and Coast Guard. The third major producer at the time was Piasecki with his tandem-rotor HRP-1.

*Montage of US
helicopter designs of the
1950s; (from top):
Sikorsky S-51, licence
built in the US as the
Dragonfly; Sikorsky
S-52, served the US Navy
and US Marine Corps as
the HO5S-1; Bell 47/
H-13, the forerunner of
6000 light helicopters;
Piesecki HRP-1, the
classic flying banana.*

Designers in Europe had also been busy during this period. In Britain, three helicopters became operational in the military: the Bristol Sycamore, the Cierva Skeeter, and the Westland Dragonfly – a version of the Sikorsky S-51.

In France, several prototypes had been built and flown, but none reached production until 1956 when both the Allouette II and the Djinn were delivered to the French Army.

*The Bristol Sycamore (above) pioneered much British military helicopter technology. (***Paul Beaver collection***)*

*Westland's first licence agreement with Sikorsky was for the Dragonfly (centre), a British version of the S-51. (***Paul Beaver collection***)*

*The Saro Skeeter, (below) a Cierva design, gave the British Army its first real helicopter for battlefield reconnaissance. This is the Skeeter AOP Mk12, pictured at AACC Middle Wallop (UK). (***Museum of Army Flying***)*

*France has become the world's largest exporter of helicopters through the Helicopter Division of Aerospatiale, formed in 1970. Amongst the designs which the state-owned combine inherited was the Sud-Est SE 3130 Alouette II. More than 1000 were built between 1957–1975.* **(Paul Beaver collection)**

# Trial by Fire

On June 25, 1950 when the North Korean Army suddenly invaded South Korea, the US military had several hundred helicopters on hand for use in its subsequent 'police action' on behalf of the United Nations. Before this war was over in l953, they had been joined by hundreds of the larger Sikorsky H-19s and Piasecki H-21s. Most of the helicopter action in the Korean War was in the role of support vehicles replacing trucks, jeeps, and ambulances in a road-poor terrain. The success of the helicopter in these roles changed the tactics and strategy of land warfare forever.

The concept of 'vertical envelopment' had been born. Little was done during this war to make the helicopter into an aggressive attack vehicle; in fact many pilots were opposed to arming their helicopters, possibly because these early aircraft often had only marginal performance to start with.

The British used their helicopters in a series of operations in Cyprus, Kenya, and Malaya where hot, moist weather provided the opportunity to learn a great deal about helicopters in less-than-optimum conditions.

*Helicopters like this Westland Wessex were vital to the British and Commonwealth victory against terrorism in Malaya.* **(Paul Beaver collection)**

*The helicopter's baptism of fire was Korea where the Bell H-13 helped save thousands of lives.*

support roles, but some were armed with guns and rockets to make them into offensive aircraft.

# Entering the Turbine Age

The USA entered the Vietnam conflict in 1961 with essentially the same type of helicopters that the French had used in Algeria but before it was over in 1975, the makeup of every nation's military helicopter fleet had been forever changed by two significant developments: the turboshaft power plant and helicopters designed specifically for the attack mission.

The turboshaft engine was a technological fall-out of the jet engines used on aeroplanes since the Second World War. By placing a turbine behind the jet, rotary power could be extracted and used to drive a propeller or a helicopter rotor. As they rapidly developed, it became clear that a turboshaft engine could replace the reciprocating engine with less than half the engine weight. This was attractive for aeroplanes but even more so for helicopters since the weight saving could be used directly for increasing the payload. As a result, since about 1960, all new military helicopters have been designed with this power plant.

Helicopters in Vietnam were at first used as they had been in Korea; primarily as troop transports and as ambulances. It soon became clear, however, that there was a need for suppression from the air of the Viet Cong who could take effective cover in the jungles and fields of tall grass and ambush the troop helicopters while in their vulnerable landing

*A Westland Scout demonstrates its versatility during the South Atlantic conflict, 1982.*

Several years later, the French became involved in an insurrection in Algeria and took the development of helicopter tactics to a high level. Not only were their 600 helicopters used in

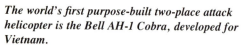

*The world's first purpose-built two-place attack helicopter is the Bell AH-1 Cobra, developed for Vietnam.*

*The US Army's first turbine helicopter was the Bell UH-1, seen here in the later UH-1H form.*

*The Hughes OH-6, seen here used for trials, was the main scout helicopter in Vietnam.*

operations. At first, the need was met by equipping some of the troop transports such as the Bell HU-1 (later UH-1) Huey with guns and rockets, but it was soon recognised that an aircraft specifically designed for the attack mission would be more effective. To meet the challenge, Bell modified their HU-1 into the AH-1, Huey Cobra by designing a slim, two-man fuselage and equipping it with a gun turret and wings on which rocket pods could be mounted.

A smaller helicopter, the Hughes OH-6 was extensively used as a scout and as a search and rescue aircraft.

*Specialised search and rescue helicopters were developed in Vietnam, such as the Sikorsky HH-53 Jolly Green Giant.* **(Paul Beaver collection)**

*Below: Boeing's versatile CH-47 Chinook medium support helicopter first saw active service in Vietnam.*

*The Lockheed Cheyenne was designed for battlefield interdiction but cancelled after a change of US policy.*

Three larger helicopters: the Sikorsky CH-53 and H-3 and the Boeing-Vertol CH-47, were found useful for search and rescue and for lifting very large loads such as artillery weapons and downed aircraft.

Later, two short conflicts, in the Falklands and in Grenada were made even shorter through the use of helicopters.

In the early 1960s, the threat of massive Warsaw Pact tank formations inspired the development in the West of helicopters primarily as tank-destroyers. The first of these was the Lockheed AH-56 Cheyenne, a high-speed compound helicopter. The project produced a small number of prototypes but was cancelled for an accumulation of technical and non-technical reasons before full-scale production could be started.

The US Army was able to recover from this in the 1970s by lowering their sights to get a somewhat less ambitious project underway to produce the Hughes (now McDonnell Douglas) AH-64 Apache.

## Developments in Other Arenas

Not only have the armies of the world found the helicopter useful on land, but the navies have

*The McDonnell Douglas Apache entered service in 1985 as the world's most advanced attack helicopter.*

*Minesweeping with a Sikorsky MH-53E Sea Dragon towing a special mine clearance sled.*

*A Westland Sea King HAS 5 of the UK Royal Navy demonstrates the use of dipping sonar for anti-submarine warfare.*

*The US Navy and US Marine Corps uses large numbers of tandem-rotor U/CH-46 Sea Knight transport helicopters.*

found that they can not do without it at sea. Dipping a stationary sonar detector has proved to be effective for discovering submarines and plotting their course.

As plane guards, helicopters have greatly increased the confidence of aircraft carrier pilots by their ability to quickly pull them from the water in case of an accident. Some types of minesweeping can be done swiftly and safely by towing submersible devices to set off mines triggered by contact, pressure, noise, or changes in the magnetic field.

The Marines have almost totally replaced their vulnerable landing craft with cargo helicopters that can overfly the beach by 10 or 100 m (19 or 185 km) to completely change the possibilities of sea-to-land assault.

With further study of this role, the US Marine Corps found that they needed a higher-speed, longer-range tactical transport to fully exploit their concept of vertical envelopment and embarked on the project resulting in the Bell/Boeing V-22 Osprey tilt-rotor aircraft.

*The V-22 Osprey represents the most ambitious converti-plane project yet. First flight in March 1989.*

All during this era from 1945 to the present, the helicopter development in the West has been paralleled by helicopter development in the Soviet Union. In some cases, such as very large helicopters, the Soviets forged ahead with their 120 000 lb (54 432 kg) Mi-26 outweighing by far the largest in the West, the 70 000 lb (31 752 kg) Sikorsky CH-53E.

The Soviets have also developed their own version of the attack helicopter in the form of the Mi-24.

*The world's largest helicopter is the Mil Mi-26 with the capacity of a C-130 cargo plane.*

*The Mi-24, seen here in a special training version, is a dynamic flying artillery weapon in widespread Soviet and Warsaw Pact service.*

Their naval requirements are met with the Kamov co-axial helicopters, the Ka-25 and Ka-27.

Although not yet having real experience, all operators of military helicopters are anticipating their eventual use in air-to-air combat by testing existing helicopters in mock engagements and using the knowledge gained to specify the characteristics of the next generation. If we are lucky, they will never be used!

*Kamov OKB specialises in co-axial helicopter rotor designs, especially for naval helicopters, such as the Ka-32.*

# Missions, Requirements and Desires

Users of existing helicopters are best able to provide guidance for the designers of new helicopters. They know what cannot be done now and can identify what needs to be done in the future.

A military requirement for a new helicopter usually starts informally as somebody might muse: 'Why don't they. . .?' Sometimes the musing begins with the recognition of a mission for which the ideal aircraft does not yet exist. At other times it is the invention of a new mission to be done by modifying an existing aircraft (an approach often followed by those with a proprietary interest in the existing aircraft). Either way, with the right protagonists and a little bit of luck, the development cycle can take on a formal life of its own.

The first step in the development of a new military helicopter is to carefully define its roles and missions in order to be able to justify the programme to those who must eventually pay for it. Except perhaps in time of war, any new programme must at least have the appearance of cost effectiveness in order to survive the repeated scrutiny to which it will be subjected. Once accepted as a viable programme within the military establishment, the helicopter industry will be formally invited to participate by responding to a 'Request for Proposal' (RFP). A typical RFP defines the requirements for the new helicopter, primarily in terms of performance both as an aircraft and as a complete system but also in many other fields such as flying qualities, survivability, maintainability, and component lives.

It should be noted that in the past a number of successful military helicopters have been developed outside this system by companies willing to risk their own resources in anticipation that military support would eventually be forthcoming. This type of effort will probably be seen less in the future as helicopter development programmes become more and more expensive.

## Performance Requirements

The usual reason a new helicopter is to be developed is to achieve a level of performance higher than that of existing aircraft. The RFP will therefore specify the required payload, speed, range or endurance, and hover performance. In addition to these primary requirements, several specific mission requirements will usually also be stated by the RFP as will be discussed in detail later.

Either stated or implied will be the allowable choice of engines. The list will usually be limited to those which are already in production or at least far enough along in their development, running in a test cell, to be viable. Engines historically take longer to develop than the airframes they power.

### Payload

The term 'payload' comes from the commercial side of aviation where it relates to the number of passengers or the amount of cargo that can be flown for a fee. In the military, the equivalent of these two items is also joined by the amount of expendable ordnance that can be carried. In some special applications, such as a scout or an anti-submarine helicopter, a suite of mechanical and/or electronic components referred to as the 'mission equipment package' (MEP) may also be counted as payload although more-or-less permanently installed in the helicopter. For some missions, the ability to carry cargo externally on a sling is required and the specifications may distinguish between the internal and external payload capabilities.

### Speed Capability

The primary justification for a helicopter is its ability to hover or to operate from very small or unimproved sites. It flies forward primarily to go from one hovering location to another. Thus the advantage of high speed is primarily to shorten the transit time. Conventional helicopters are limited by inherent aerodynamic phenomena to maximum forward speeds of about 200 kts (370 km/h). Any requirement above that speed will force the designers to consider variations such as a compound helicopter with a wing and auxiliary propulsion or a tilt rotor aircraft. Each of these carry inherent cost and weight penalties over the conventional helicopter. Even when speed requirements are less than 200 kts (370 km/h), the exact value will determine whether the hover or the high speed requirement will be the critical one in matching the aircraft design to the available engine.

## Range or Endurance

The proposed mission of the aircraft will prompt the customer to specify either the maximum range or the maximum endurance. Sometimes, the critical mission is a combination of these at various speeds and flight conditions. In any case, these are the requirements from which the weight of required fuel is calculated. Besides determining the capacity of the internal fuel tanks, this has a significant effect on the size of the helicopter since at least one pound of structure is required to support each additional pound of useful load.

If a long range ferry mission is also specified, it will determine the size of any auxiliary fuel tanks for which provision must be made. For world-wide self-deployment, the minimum required ferry ranges are 1260 nm (2335 km) for an Atlantic crossing and 2100 nm (3900 km) for the Pacific. The RFP might not give the designer the option of providing an in-flight refueling capability, but it probably will give him some size requirements for transportation of a certain number of his helicopters in a specified cargo aeroplane.

## Hover or Vertical Rate of Climb

Helicopters need to be able to hover or to climb vertically at design gross weight with adequate performance under extreme environmental conditions. Recent US Army requirements as applied to both the Sikorsky UH-60 utility transport and to the McDonnell Douglas AH-64 attack helicopter specified that these machines demonstrate a vertical rate of climb of 450 ft/min (2.25 m/sec) at the take-off gross weight for their design

mission at an altitude of 4000 ft (1219 m) and 95°F (35°C) with only 95 per cent of the 30 minutes power rating (Intermediate Power) of their engines for these conditions. This altitude and temperature combination is thought to cover almost all possible world-wide situations. The 95 per cent limit is to account for normal engine deterioration with use and the specified vertical rate of climb of 450 ft/min was chosen as a reasonable operational manoeuvre.

Helicopters procured for US Navy operations are usually required to do their hovering on a 'Navy Hot Day' corresponding to an altitude of 3000 ft (914 m) and 91.5°F (33°C).

# Stability and Control

The RFP may not implicitly specify the requirements for flying qualities. It may, instead, refer to a separate military specification for compliance. Since 1951, this document usually has been the US specification, MIL-H-8501A *Helicopter Flying and Ground Handling Qualities*. At this writing, this document is being revised and may acquire a different designation. Because parts of MIL-H-8501A were considered obsolete in the 1970s, the RFPs for the US Army's UTTAS and AAH programmes which resulted in the Sikorsky H-60 and the McDonnell Douglas AH-64 included special up-dated versions of it for compliance.

# Reliability, Availability and Maintainability

A group of considerations known as the 'ilities' have always been important but have only recently been raised from the designer's subconscious to his conscious mind. These include reliability, availability and maintainability. As a group, they are known as 'RAM'. The motivation has come from the customer who often saw more problems in these aspects than in performance, flying qualities, or structural integrity where the designer had traditionally placed the bulk of his effort.

### Reliability

Reliability is quantified by reference to the 'Mean Time Between Failures' (MTBF) for both individual components and for the system as a whole. Sometimes, the definition is more specific; for instance, as 'Mean Time Between Mission

Affecting Failures'. Typical values initially proposed for the US Army's LHX programme for this type of failure were 8.4 flight hours for the Scout/Attack version (SCAT) and 14.5 hours for the Utility version (light transport). Many of the components that are of concern here will be supplied by vendors, but the prime contractor must accept full responsibility for each unless it is 'Government Furnished Equipment' (GFE) and even here, the designer must consider its interface with his aircraft by providing such amenities as adequate structural support and cooling.

## Availability

Although availability is the next of the three RAM 'ilities', it depends on the other two. It is a measure of what percentage of the time the helicopter will be ready to perform its role. The requirements may be different depending on whether the helicopter is being flown in peacetime or in wartime. The initial LHX requirements for peacetime in which the aircraft were expected to fly only 240 hours per year were 86 per cent for the SCAT and 90 per cent for the Utility. The corresponding requirements for wartime in which the machines would be expected to fly at the hectic rate of 2200 hours per year were 72 per cent for SCAT and 80 per cent for the LHX-U.

## Maintainability

Maintainability is measured by the number of scheduled and non-scheduled man-hours of maintenance per flight hour. It includes both 'direct maintenance' and the time to make repairs due to component failures and also due to combat damage. The initial LHX requirement for direct maintenance was 2.6 man-hours per flight hour for SCAT and 2.4 for the Utility version. Even the time to make a repair in the field was specified; being not more than 2 hours (more extensive repair work was to be done at the depot level).

Achieving ambitious goals such as these requires two capabilities: a quick diagnostic procedure to identify problems; and a rapid means of replacing components. The first may be assisted by automatic testing equipment both on board the helicopter and on the ground using elements of a Fault Detection/Location System (FD/LS). The second goal is achieved by packaging components as quick-change modules.

Another aspect of maintainability is component life. Because of the hard usage that many helicopter components experience, some may have to be replaced after a certain number of hours. If that time is short, much of the maintenance effort will be expended in exchanging one component for a new one. The requirements for the UH-60 and the AH-64 were that many component lives had to be at least 4500 hours. Others were to be so easily inspected that they could be replaced 'on condition'.

# Survivability

Survivability has three aspects. One is the ability to fly undetected by your adversary. The second is the ability to take effective evasive action once detected, and the third is the ability to protect the crew and the aircraft if the enemy fires weapons. In that case, it not only entails the ability to absorb punishment without failing but to also protect the crew in a crash.

## Stealth

Military operations often rely on surprise for their effectiveness. For aircraft of all types, this means 'stealth', or having 'low observable' characteristics. We observe with our natural senses, sometimes enhanced, and with any artificial senses we can muster. The ways a helicopter can signal its approach or presence to the enemy are through sight, sound, radar return, and infra-red or electromagnetic emissions. The RFP for a combat helicopter will put limits on the sound signature for various flight conditions, and on the maximum radar cross-section and infra-red emission. The latter two not only affect the detection distance but also how good a target the helicopter is to radar-directed guns and heat-seeking missiles.

## Evasive Manoeuvring

Any helicopter used in the combat zone must be capable of effective evasive manoeuvring no matter what its intended role is. The most important factor in this regard is the amount of excess power available over that just required for steady flight. This is the basis of the vertical rate of climb specification for modern military helicopters. In an emergency, the pilot should be able to make use of all of the available engine power without being concerned with structural or transmission limits. The second most important factor is turning capability. At slow speeds, this depends on the thrust margin of the tail rotor but at most forward speeds, it depends on the roll acceleration and roll rate characteristics and on the maximum load factor that can be developed. All of these will be specified in the RFP but beyond that, the pilot should have the confidence that he can use all of the manoeuvring capabilities without worrying about causing immediate structural damage.

## Crashworthiness

The RFP will specify crashworthiness by defining the amount of 'living room' that must remain around the occupants after a crash for a number of specified impact angles and velocities. For the same conditions, the maximum allowable acceleration at the seats will be specified. These two requirements guide the engineer in providing a crash-survivable environment. Other requirements will specify the capability of the fuel tanks to survive a crash without contributing to a post-crash fire.

# Crew Comfort

A tired and uncomfortable pilot will not be able to function as well as a comfortable one and even for passengers, comfort is an important consideration. The RFP will address this question in several ways. Putting limits on internal noise and vibration and specifiying the upper and lower boundaries of cockpit and cabin temperature are two examples. Recent work on seat geometry for helicopters is expected to lead to seat designs that are comfortable to the point where the pilot is not distracted by stiff muscles or hot spots. Requirements on field-of-view and on cockpit lighting for night flying are also a normal part of a new RFP.

# Vulnerability

Any helicopter that must go into a battle zone must be designed with vulnerability in mind. For this reason, the RFP will specify the threat and the maximum 'vulnerable area' to that threat. For example, the AH-64 requirement is that no single 12.7mm (50 calibre) round will do enough damage to prevent the helicopter from returning safely to its base; i.e. the vulnerable area to this threat is zero. It also is desired that maximum protection be provided for even larger projectiles. Designers have several options for achieving goals like these. They can provide redundancy for all critical systems and structures, including the pilot; provide 'parasitic' armour; shield critical components with other less critical components; or make individual parts 'ballistic tolerant'. Transmissions may be required to survive loss of lubrication for periods up to half an hour and fuel tanks may be required to be self-sealing. Protection against natural dangers such as ice, lightning, and bird strikes will also be specified. For helicopters expected to operate in high-risk areas in future warfare, there may be requirements spelled out for protection against chemicals, biological agents, and radiation (CBR).

# Mission Requirements

## Small Transports

A utility helicopter with the capability to carry six to eight soldiers or the equivalent in cargo will always be needed. At one time, the US Marines were interested in one-man helicopters that were to be used by one combat soldier to cross a river or to quickly fly into the enemy's rear area. They even bought prototypes for testing from Hiller and from Gyrodyne. It soon became apparent, however, that the concept had only limited applications. It meant training all US Marines as helicopter pilots and in a combat situation losing most of the machines on the first operation as their pilot/soldiers abandoned them to do more important things. Thus the typical small transport now has at least one full-time proprietor whose primary duty is to transport several people or several hundred pounds of cargo. Other duties for these aircraft include observation, battlefield command and control, search and rescue, and casualty evacuation. Its role is presently being filled by the Bell OH-58, the Westland Lynx, the Aerospatiale Gazelle, and the MBB BO 105.

## Medium Transports

These helicopters are large enough to transport 15 to 30 soldiers with the ability to rapidly discharge them in the battle area. Alternatively, they can carry five to ten tonnes of cargo either internally or as an underslung load. In this category today are the Sikorsky UH-60, the Boeing CH-46, the Aerospatiale Super Puma, the Mi-8 'Hip', and the EH 101.

## Large Transports

Since the military have some large pieces of equipment such as tanks that are sometimes frustrated by terrain features, large helicopters are desirable to provide a timely lift. As a rule-of-thumb, a modern helicopter can lift a load equal to about half its maximum gross weight. It is now feasible, however, to lift one load with more than one helicopter so that future requirements for giant machines may be by-passed. For transporting people who come in convenient 200 lb (91 kg) packages, it is less important to use very large helicopters although they are cost effective if the consolidated loads are large enough; just as commercial airlines find motivation in buying very large transport aircraft. Helicopters of this type include the Sikorsky CH-53, the Boeing CH-47, and the Mi-26.

## Scouts

The primary purpose of a scout/observation/reconnaissance helicopter is to search the battle zone for targets worthy of larger and more heavily armed attack helicopters and aeroplanes. As such, it should be small to minimise detection but equipped with all of the sensors that can be used to carry out its task not only in good visual conditions but also at night and in bad weather. It probably should be armed only to the degree necessary to protect itself when unexpectedly fired upon. A current example in US Army service is the Bell OH-58D.

## Attack

For carrying an aggressive fire capability to the enemy with special emphasis on the anti-tank role this helicopter should be heavily armed and armoured. It also should have an all-weather day/night capability.

Today, attack helicopters are taken to be the most advanced and capable armed helicopters with a primary role of engaging enemy armour and strong points, often from stand-off range or behind the Forward Line of Enemy Troops (FLET). In the West, the only production aircraft which currently fulfil this role are the Bell AH-1E SuperCobra and AH-64A Apache. New generation types will include the Eurocopter

HAC/PAH-2 developments of the CATH programme.

Other variants of the attack helicopter are the Light Attack Helicopter (LAH) with a lesser level of combat capability for defensive operations in the withdrawal in contact phase of a land battle. The European and US standard for LAH is a tandem seating arrangement, with examples such as the Bell AH-1F/S Cobra and Agusta A 129A Mangusta.

Anti-Tank Helicopters are now considered to be former utility and liaison which have been optimised as interim helicopters for armed action against enemy armoured fighting vehicles. Types include the Lynx/TOW, BO 105/HOT, Gazelle/HOT, MD500/TOW and older types, such as the Alouette III/AS 12.

## Air-To-Air

At this writing, little actual helicopter dog-fighting experience has been reported, although much has been done in test environments using non-lethal means of scoring. A helicopter equipped for this role must be armed with the appropriate weapons, usually both guns or missiles, and be manoeuverable enough to make use of them in the most advantageous manner. After the first pass, almost all of the test engagements have developed into a slow-speed 'knife fight in a telephone booth' with the adversaries trying to out-turn and out-climb each other to get into that favoured position of behind and above. Thus a high rate of climb and the ability to make rapid turns are two of the basic requirements. Speed itself seems to be an advantage only in getting to the scene of the action, and since speed requirements of much over 200 kts (370 km/h) will impose penalties with respect to weight and cost, how to make this trade-off can only be done with a clear crystal ball. These helicopters will also have an escort role.

## Anti-Submarine Warfare

This category is one of the few where the customer may specify a mission endurance as well as a mission range. Hovering while dipping a sonar detector is one of the basic elements of this role. Overwater flying always justifies a multi-engine design, and three engines may be more practical than two to provide 'one-engine-inoperative' (OEI) safety during the hover portion of a mission. Despite this assurance, these aircraft must be designed with ditching in mind and a requirement will be established to remain afloat for a reasonable length of time in a specified sea state (wave height/wind strength).

The RFP for a shipborne helicopter will also specify the handling and storage requirements in terms of the size of the hanger and/or lifts with which the aircraft must be compatible. For operation on many types of ships, the deck-handling characteristics in terms of roll-over angles and compatibility with landing-assist systems will be specified.

Any aircraft that must operate close to salt water must have special attention given to anti-corrosion protection. This generally means that such corrosion-prone materials as magnesium that are satisfactory for land-based aircraft are unacceptable for those operating at sea. Another special consideration for shipborne aircraft is protection from the high energy electro-magnetic sources such as search radars that warships carry. Precautions have to be included in the design to protect the helicopter's avionic equipment and to insolate electrically-primed ammunition from these effects. A final special requirement for safe operation aboard ships is automatic or quick and fool-proof manual blade folding.

## Search and Rescue

The search and rescue (SAR) role like that of the anti-submarine helicopter requires good and safe hovering capability since many actual rescues will be done from hover. For those engaged in naval operations, the ability to safely ditch in the sea is a requirement. The size of the cabin will be dictated by how many survivors are to be carried and what type of care they will require on the return to base. Speed, range and endurance will be determined by the anticipated conditions of the role. Combat-rescue helicopters need enhanced survivability equipment packages.

## Anti-Surface Vessel Warface

Helicopters can be armed for specialised surface search, identification and anti-ship tasks. Very similar characteristics to that of the ASW helicopter are required as well as the ability to operate compatible guided weapons.

## Trainer

Most people coming into the military can drive cars but practically none of them can fly helicopters. Even if they could, the services would insist that they learn to fly in a standard manner so there will always be a need for helicopter training. Primary trainers need not be much different than their civilian counterparts, but advanced trainers will have to have features of the operational helicopters to make training meaningful. As a matter of fact, they will probably be nothing less than the operational machines themselves.

# A Brief Review of Helicopter Aerodynamics

Before embarking on the description of the design process, it seems well to review some of the aerodynamic principles that both guide and constrain the helicopter designer.

## Hover

### Wake Characteristics

Like any physical system, the hovering helicopter must obey the basic laws of physics. One of these was stated by Newton: 'For every action, there is an equal and opposite reaction'. In the case of the hovering helicopter, the action is the development of a rotor thrust equal to the gross weight. The reaction is represented by the acceleration of a mass of air from a stagnant condition far above the rotor to a condition with finite velocity in the wake below the rotor.

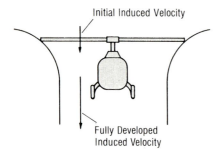

*Wake of a Hovering Helicopter*

It may be shown by considering both the momentum and the kinetic energy in the system that the induced velocity in the mature wake is twice that at the rotor disc. The figure below shows the induced velocity in the wake generated by several current helicopters. As may be seen, helicopters with the highest disc loadings come closest to producing hurricane-like downwash velocities that can generate visibility problems while hovering over loose surfaces and can make working under a hovering helicopter difficult.

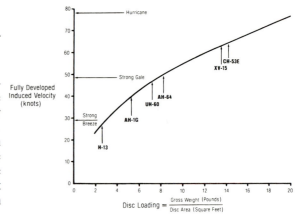

*Velocity in the Wake*

### Figure of Merit

High disc loadings not only affect downwash velocities, but the power required to hover as well. This is shown on a plot of power loading – which is the pounds of thrust per horsepower – versus disc loading.

The plot shows three lines representing different values of the 'Figure of Merit'. This is the ratio of the theoretical minimum power to the power actually required and as such is a measurement of hovering efficiency. A Figure of Merit of 1.0 is the best a rotor can do without violating the laws of physics. It could theoretically be achieved by an ideal rotor with no blade drag nor other losses. The line for a Figure of Merit of 0.8 represents a good 'state of the art' rotor designed primarily for hover and the line for 0.6 represents a rotor that has also been designed to

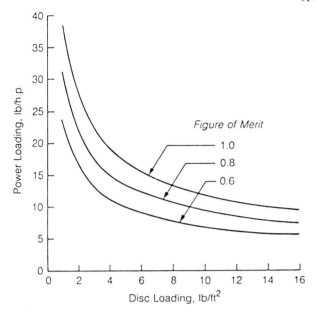

**Main Rotor Hover Performance**

give good performance at high speed resulting in a performance compromise at hover.

## Blade Element Theory

The momentum considerations with which we have been dealing have value in providing a partial understanding of hover, but to go further, we need to examine what is happening at the blade itself. The velocities and forces associated with an element of the blade are shown below.

The rotational velocity and the induced velocity combine vectorially to produce the resultant velocity which has a definite downward slope. Since lift is perpendicular to the resultant

velocity, it is tilted aft and its horizontal component is called 'induced drag'. The engine must overcome this as well as the profile drag caused by air friction on the surface of the blade and the blade pitch must be high enough to produce an angle of attack with respect to the resultant velocity in order to generate the required lift.

The lift and drag on the blade element depend on the angle of attack of the airfoil section.

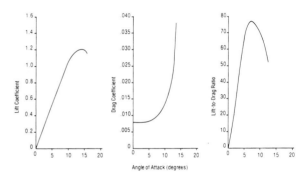

**Typical Airfoil Characteristics**

To obtain the best hover performance, the airfoil should be flown at the angle of attack that gives the highest lift-to-drag ratio which is about seven degrees for the airfoil shown. This is where the highest Figure of Merit is achieved.

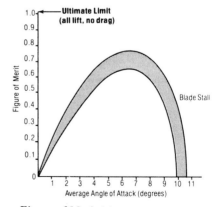

**Hover Figure of Merit (a)**

The Blade Loading Co-efficient: Helicopter aerodynamicists, like aeroplane aerodynamicists, find it convenient to work with non-dimensional

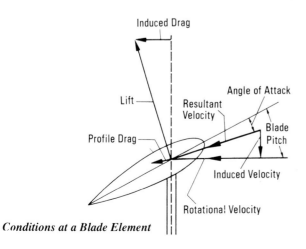

**Conditions at a Blade Element**

coefficients. The one which has the most effect on preliminary design is the blade loading coefficient, $C_T/\sigma$, whose equation is:

$$C_T/\sigma = \frac{\text{Thrust}}{\text{Air Density} \times \text{Blade Area} \times \text{Tip Speed}^2}$$

This coefficient is related to the average lift coefficient and thus to the average angle of attack. This is shown in a replot of the Figure of Merit curve, this time as a function of $C_T/\sigma$.

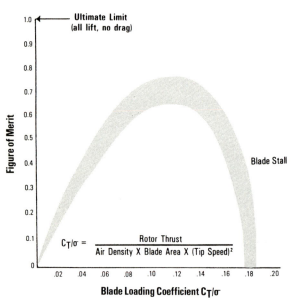

*Hover Figure of Merit (b)*

One of the factors that will be chosen during the preliminary design is the operating value of this coefficient. It may be seen that it has a strong effect on the hovering efficiency. It will also be shown that it has an equally strong effect on the ability to fly at high forward speeds.

# Vertical Climbs and Descents

Besides hovering, the helicopter can go straight up and straight down. This introduces new considerations into the aerodynamics of the rotor. As might be expected, it takes more power to climb than to hover. If the helicopter were an elevator, the additional power would be strictly proportional to the rate of change of its potential energy. A helicopter, however, can take advantage of the extra mass flow through the rotor and the result is that the extra power to ascend vertically is only half what it would be for an elevator.

The same thing applies to descent – as long as it is a slow descent. If, however, the rate of descent is about as much as the normal downflow through the rotor required to produce thrust, the flow conditions are such that the air is going both up and down through and around the rotor in a disorganised manner. This is called the 'vortex ring' state. Wind tunnel tests using smoke for flow visualisation indicate that the rotor appears to be pumping air into a big bubble that fills up and periodically bursts as shown below.

Both the magnitude and direction of the rotor thrust undergo massive fluctuations during this condition. When the rate of descent reaches about twice the normal hovering inflow velocity, the flow once again stabilises as it passes up through the rotor. In this condition, the rotor is in autorotation, requiring no power to keep turning and producing thrust.

Not only is the main rotor subject to the vortex ring state, but so is the tail rotor in left sideward flight (on helicopters whose main rotors are turning counter-clockwise when viewed from above). For many helicopters the tail rotor is subject to the flow fluctuations of the vortex ring state at sideward speeds of between 15 and 40 knots (28 to 74 km/h).

*Vortex Ring Conditions*

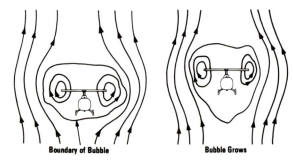

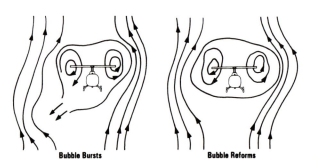

# Forward Flight

Just as in hover, there are two methods of analysing the characteristics of a rotor in forward flight: the momentum, or energy method; and the blade element method. The momentum method provides a rapid means of obtaining a first estimate of the performance as well as a valuable insight into the physics of the system but the blade element method is necessary for accurate performance estimation and for establishing the limits of rotor performance.

## Trim Conditions

The balance of forces that governs the helicopter in forward flight is shown below.

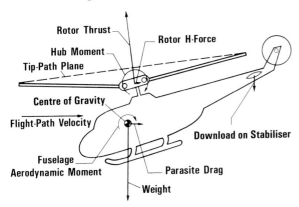

*Trim in Forward Flight*

The rotor thrust vector must balance not only the gross weight, as it does in hover, but also the horizontal forces due to the drag of the rotor blades and the drag of the fuselage, hub, landing gear, and other components of the aircraft. The drag of the rotor blades is known as the rotor horizontal force or H-force, and all other drag items are classified as 'parasite drag'.

The H-force in the plane of the rotor disc is caused by the differential drag on the blades on the advancing and retreating sides. Drag on the advancing side acts aft, but drag on the retreating side acts forward, like an oar in water. Thus the H-force is usually relatively small but can be of either sign.

Not only do all of the horizontal and vertical forces need to be balanced, but so do all of the moments about the centre of gravity. On modern helicopters, this is done by giving the pilot control of the amount of flapping that the rotor has with respect to the airframe.

## Momentum Theory

Because the rotor in forward flight is experiencing more mass flow than in hover, it does not have to work so hard on the passing air to produce lift. This reduces the induced velocity exactly as if it were a wing. When a wing flies past, it theoretically disturbs all the air in the neighborhood from far above to far below and to both sides. Of course, it is the air closest to the flight path that is influenced most, but the generality still holds. When the mathematics of the problem are worked out, it may be shown that moving all of that air in varying amounts is exactly the same as if every molecule of air in a cylindrical stream tube whose diameter is equal to the wingspan were given the same value of downward velocity. This mathematical fiction is also the correct way to think of a rotor in forward flight and means that by coincidence, an area equal to the rotor disc is the key parameter for induced power calculations in both hover and forward flight.

As the helicopter goes faster, there is more air going through the stream tube and the rotor has to do less work on it to maintain constant thrust. For this reason, induced power decreases with speed until for most helicopters at maximum speed, it is one-quarter or less of its hover value. This is shown in the figure below which also shows the other power components.

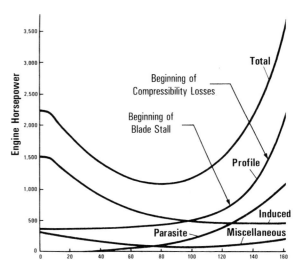

*Elements of Power Required in Forward Flight*

The power required to overcome the drag due to friction on the blades is called 'profile power'. It accounts for 15 to 40 per cent of the main rotor power in hover and remains at a fairly constant level as the helicopter goes into forward flight since increases on the advancing side tend to be compensated for by decreases on the retreating side until at high speed when blade stall or compressibility, or both, become important.

The power required to overcome the drag of all the aircraft components except the rotor blades is 'parasite power'. It is of no consequence at low speed (except to produce a download when the fuselage is immersed in the rotor wake at hover) but since it increases as forward speed cubed, it becomes important at high speeds. This power is proportional to the helicopter's 'equivalent flat plate drag area', which depends upon the size and the general cleanliness of the aircraft.

The engine has to put out enough power to provide for the induced, profile, and parasite power components and for some others that can be lumped together under a 'miscellaneous' heading including those associated with the tail rotor, gearboxes, hydraulic pumps, electrical generators, etc. When all the various types of power are added up, a picture is obtained of the total power required for steady, level flight. One of the most important characteristics of this curve is that, until flying very fast, a helicopter takes less power to fly forward than to hover. Another characteristic is that the curve starts out with zero slope because the rotor cannot distinguish between small forward and small rearward speeds.

## Blade Element Theory

Just as in hovering, the momentum, or energy method is useful in understanding the physics of forward flight and for making rough calculations, but the blade element theory must be used to define flight limitations and to do more accurate calculations. In forward flight, the velocity acting on the blade element is a function both of the radial station and of the blade azimuth position.

The azimuth angle, $\psi$, is defined with its zero position over the tail. The velocity acting on the blade element is the vector sum of the velocity due to rotation, $\Omega r$, and the forward speed of the helicopter, $V$. The study of swept wing aerodynamics has shown that the component of velocity perpendicular to the leading edge is the only velocity that is important in establishing aerodynamic forces. Over the tail boom and over the fuselage nose, the blade elements see the

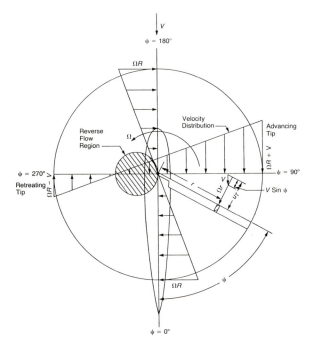

*Tangential Velocities in Forward Flight*

same velocity as in hover, but on the advancing blade they see higher velocities and on the retreating blade, lower. As a matter of fact, on the retreating blade there are elements close to the hub where the velocity perpendicular to the leading edge is actually negative, that is, the air strikes the trailing edge first.

## Blade Flapping

The asymmetry of the velocity distribution is a dominant factor in the forward flight of helicopters and accounts for most of the differences between helicopters and aeroplanes. Compared to the wing of an aeroplane, the rotor of a helicopter appears to be, at best, only loosely connected to its aircraft. The idea of flexibly attaching rotor blades to the hub was developed in the 1920s as an engineering fix by Juan de la Cierva, the designer of the autogiro. The autogiro is a rotary-wing aircraft that unlike the helicopter has no power going to the rotor, but relies on its windmilling characteristics to keep it turning while being pulled through the air by a propeller.

On Cierva's first autogiros, the blades were rigidly braced to the shaft using wires, and the asymmetry of the velocities caused them to roll over during taxi. When Cierva installed hinges that permitted the blades to flap, the resulting motion caused by the asymmetricity produced an alleviating effect. The blade on the advancing side rose and in so doing experienced a decrease in its angle of attack. The opposite thing happened on the retreating side. As a result, the flapping motion cyclically changed the angle of attack just enough to compensate for the asymmetry of the velocities. With this fix, Cierva was able to successfully develop his aircraft. The presence of a flapping hinge, or at least a moderate amount of flexibility, has been a standard feature of all rotary-wing aircraft since then.

Cierva also introduced the lead-lag hinge to permit the blade to find its natural position in the rotor plane to reduce in-plane moments that had given him structural problems on his early autogiros.

## Helicopter Control System

On the early autogiros, the nose-up flapping of the rotor produced a nose-up pitching moment that was balanced with an aeroplane-type elevator controlled by the pilot. Helicopters do not have elevators. Instead, they rely on a control system that can cyclically vary the pitch around the disc so that it is reduced on the advancing side and increased on the retreating side. The pilot using fore and aft motion of his 'cyclic' stick puts in the right magnitude to keep the rotor in aero-

*Pitcairn Autogiro.*

dynamic balance. At the same time, he is also generating just enough flapping to make the moments about the centre of gravity equal to zero. (For most helicopters with the centre of gravity near the rotor shaft, only a few degrees of flapping is required.) If he wants to manoeuvre, he can use the cyclic system to tilt the rotor. In addition, the pilot has a 'collective' stick that changes the pitch of all the blades by the same amount at the same time thus allowing him to generate the right amount of thrust for trim and to go up and down.

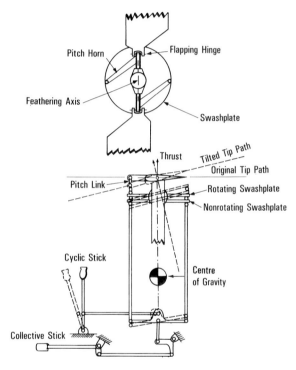

*Cyclic and Collective Control Systems*

## Maximum Thrust

There is a limit to how much balancing can be done with cyclic pitch. At very high speeds, the retreating blade is going so slowly relative to the air that in order to develop any lift at all, it must operate at very high angles of attack. When these angles reach the stall angle of the blade, the allowable maximum speed has been reached.

Flight test and wind tunnel experiments have provided the helicopter aerodynamicists with data from which they can plot this limit in a non-dimensional form as the maximum value of the blade loading co-efficient versus the tip speed

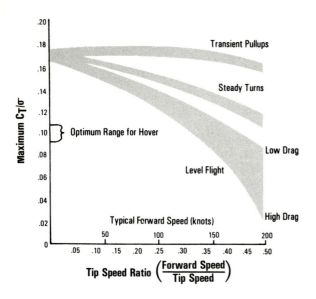

*Maximum Rotor Thrust Capabilities*

ratio, which is the ratio between forward speed and tip speed.

The limit starts out at its highest at hover. As forward flight is entered, the maximum lifting capability of the retreating blade is decreased by its lower relative air speed and to avoid unbalancing the rotor, the lift capability of the advancing blade must be artificially reduced using cyclic pitch. Thus only the blades over the nose and tail retain the same potential as in hover and so the overall lifting capability of the rotor decreases as speed increases. The lower band of the figure applies to straight and level flight. It can be used to determine the maximum

speed of a given helicopter as limited by retreating blade stall at the operating value of the blade loading co-efficient as determined by gross weight and air density.

It is worth noting that helicopter altitude records are set at very low forward speeds to take advantage of the highest possible co-efficient.

The lower band is painted with a broad brush because several secondary effects influence it. One important effect is how much the rotor tip path plane must be tilted down to overcome airframe drag. The higher the drag, the more nose-down tilt and the more adverse the angle of attack becomes on the retreating side. The amount of blade twist is also a factor since high twist will lower the angle of attack at the extreme tip which is most sensitive to stall effects. Even the dynamic characteristics of the blades will influence the perceived effects of retreating blade stall.

The middle band represents the limit during a steady turn. It is higher than in level flight because to maintain the turn, the rotor must be precessed nose-up like a gyro. To achieve this, the advancing blade is loaded higher than in level flight and this extra load accounts for the increased rotor thrust capability in a turn. The top band shows the possibility for a transient pull-up where the rotor is tilted nose-up far enough to put it into autorotation with the air flow going up through it. In this condition, the angle of attack distribution is much more favorable on the retreating side and consequently stall is much less of a problem. In this condition, too, the drag on the blade elements contribute to upward rotor thrust instead of diminishing it as it does in powered flight.

# The Preliminary Design Process

Preliminary Design is generally looked on as the most glamorous of the aircraft engineering disciplines since it is where grand schemes can be put on paper with only minimum constraints provided by consideration of details. It is generally assigned to people who have both a good sense of invention and the experience to use it in a practical way. The preliminary designer should also have a working knowledge of structures, aerodynamics and weights, or at least have specialists in each of these disciplines at his elbow.

## The One-Hour Estimate

After reviewing the requirements for a new helicopter, the preliminary design engineer begins by making 'cartoons' of possible configurations, but it is not long before he will have to make a first estimate of the size and weight. A quick start can be made using a combination of past experience and a knowledge of the basic laws of physics. Both the hover and high speed flight goals will have been stated. The objective of the initial design step will be to find the approximate combination of physical parameters for the helicopter that will simultaneously satisfy both flight regimes; that is, produce a 'balanced' design with the smallest aircraft possible. It will not, of course, be completely done in the one hour allotted for this exercise, but at the end of this time, a fairly defensible starting point will have been established.

### Requirements

As an illustration of the procedure, it is helpful to use a specific example. Let us assume that we have been asked to design a small battlefield transport helicopter with the following requirements:

| | |
|---|---|
| **Payload:** | 8 fully-equipped troops @ 220 lb (100 kg) = 1760 lb (798 kg) |
| **Crew:** | 2 pilots @ 200 lb (100 kg) = 400 lb (200 kg) |
| **Maximum Speed at Sea Level:** | 200 kts (370 km/h) at the 30 min engine rating |
| **Cruise Speed at Sea Level:** | At least 175 kts (324 km/h) at the maximum continuous engine rating |
| **Range:** | 300 nm (555 km) at continuous engine rating with 30 min fuel reserve |
| **Vertical Rate-of-Climb:** | 450 ft/min (137 m/min) @ 4000 ft (1220 m), 95°F (35°C) with 95 per cent of the 30 min rating |
| **Engines:** | Two; with sea level maximum continuous ratings of 650 hp (484 kw) each, 30 min ratings of 800 hp (596 kw) each |

### Initial Gross Weight Estimating

The first step is to estimate the fuel required to do the mission. Modern turbine engines can be assumed to have a specific fuel consumption (sfc) of about 0.5 lb (227 g) per hp/h at their continuous ratings. For the 300 nm (555 km) task at the continuous engine rating this gives an estimate for the fuel required of 1440 lb (654 kg) including the 30 min reserve. When this is added to the payload and the crew weight, the resultant 'useful load' is 3600 lbs (1633 kg).

To estimate the gross weight, previous experience summarised in the figure below may be

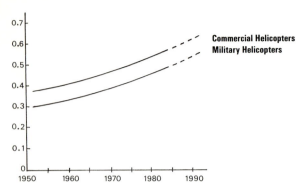

*Historic Trend of Ratio of Useful Load to Gross Weight*

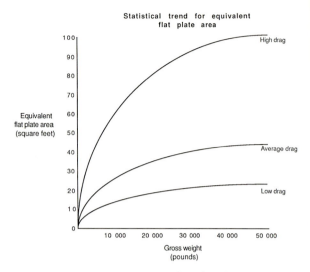

*Statistical Trend for Equivalent Flat Plate Area*

used. It is based on a study of weight trends for helicopters designed in the recent past.

Two lines are shown; one for commercial helicopters and a slightly lower one for combat helicopters that are penalised by the neccessity to carry such things as redundant components, armour protection and self-sealing fuel tanks. It may be seen that the ratio of useful load to gross weight has been steadily increasing as newer technology has been introduced into the industry. For a design of the early 1990s, the ratio for a combat helicopter should be close to 0.5 which means that as a first guess, the gross weight of our helicopter will be about 7200 lbs (3265 kg).

## Check on Maximum Forward Speed

An estimate of the high speed capability can be made using some relationships also based on previous designs. The figure shows the equivalent flat plate parasite drag area as a function of gross weight for helicopters that are considered to have three different levels of aerodynamic 'cleanliness'.

If ours has an average drag level, the curve indicates a value of 16 sq ft (4.8 m²). Assuming that 70 per cent of the installed power is being used to overcome parasite drag at high speed, the maximum speed in knots at sea level can be found from the equation:

$$\text{Max Spd} = 41\sqrt[3]{\text{30 min rating of both engines/equiv flt plt. area}}$$

For this example, with two engines rated at 800 hp (596 kW), the equation gives a maximum speed of 190 kts (352 km/h) which indicates that we either have to choose a larger engine or design a cleaner-than-average helicopter in order to achieve the required 200 kts (370 km/h). Even with the average drag level, using the maximum continuous power of 650 (485 kW) easily meets the required cruise speed of 175 kts (324 km/h).

## Sizing the Rotor

The rotor diameter is sized by the vertical rate-of-climb requirement of 450 ft/min (137 m/min) at 4000 ft (1219 m). 95°F (35°C) with 95 per cent of the 30 min rating.. It was stated in Chapter 3 that the additional power to climb vertically over that required to hover is equal to one half the rate of change in potential energy. A check on previous designs shows that the additional power for a climb rate of 450 ft/min (137 m/min) is approximately 10 per cent of the power required to hover.

The maximum output of the engine changes from its sea level, standard rating as either altitude or temperature change. A modern turbine engine loses about 30 per cent of its capability when going to 4000 ft (1219 m), 95°F (35°C).

Not only does the engine power change, but so does the power required by the rotor. As the density goes down the rotor induced power goes up while its profile power is going down.

All three of these effects have been combined into a plot of power loading (referenced to the sea level rating) versus disc loading for a conventional, single-rotor helicopter climbing vertically at 450 ft/min (137 m/min) at 4000 ft (1219 m), 95°F (35°C). For this plot, the Figure of Merit based on the entire helicopter has been taken as equal to 0.6.

The requirement is that the vertical rate-of-climb be done with 95 per cent of the 30 min rating. At sea level, this would be a total of 1520 hp (1133 kW) and since the helicopter

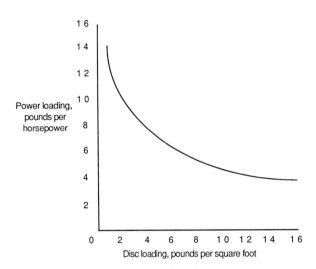

*Rotor Performance for Design Conditions*

weighs 7200 lbs (3266 kg) (for the first time around at least), the power loading to use is 4.7 lbs per hp (or 2.10 kg per kW). From the figure, this corresponds to a disc loading of 9 lb/ft$^2$ (1.8 kg/m$^2$) which for this gross weight gives a rotor radius of 16 ft (4.9 m). Thus we have a starting point.

## Computerised Preliminary Design

In many design organisations, some of the rough assumptions on which this 'one-hour' estimate was based are by-passed with a computer program containing more sophisticated ways of estimating performance, fuel flow and component weights. Although the computer cannot do anything the design engineer could not do, it can do it faster thus giving him more time to investigate options and the effects of variations in some of his design decisions. These programs will generally contain empirical performance equations for hover, forward flight, and manoeuvering. They will also include weight equations for the various structural, mechanical, and equipment components based on statistical studies of actual previous helicopters with some allowance for real or hoped-for improvements in the 'state of the art'. They will also contain first approximation methods for selecting the minimum blade area for both the main and tail rotors based on performance and manoeuvre requirements, for sizing the horizontal and vertical stabiliser surfaces, and for estimating the drag of the various components.

An engine 'deck' supplied by the engine manufacturer may be incorporated in the program to provide a realistic estimate of fuel flow based on the specific fuel consumption for each specific flight condition. This then, allows the calculation of the fuel required for hybrid missions consisting of legs that might involve hover, climb, cruise, dash, and loiter in various combinations. A block diagram for such a program is shown below.

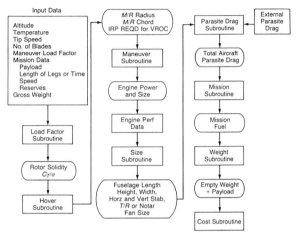

*Typical Preliminary Design Program*

The goal of most of these programs is to find the gross weight for which the allowance for the fuel available is equal to the fuel required as shown below.

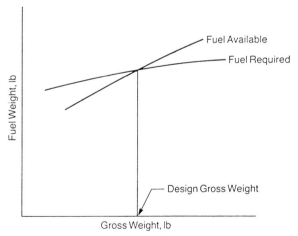

*Result of Preliminary Design Study*

# Start of the Drawings

Whether from a computerised design process or

from one based on hand calculations, we now have a starting point for the designers to begin to make their two primary drawings: the 'General Arrangement' which is a three-view drawing showing the external characteristics and the 'Inboard Profile' which is an 'X-Ray' version showing the relative arrangement of the primary internal features.

While making the inboard profile, the designer has two goals: to locate all of the expendable weight items as close to the rotor shaft as possible to minimise the centre of gravity shift with loading; and to design short and direct structural load paths between those components from which loads will originate in flight, in landing, and in a crash.

With these and the more detailed drawings that come later, the weight engineers can calculate the weight of all the individual components to refine the original estimate of the gross weight and to accurately locate the centre of gravity position. The aerodynamicists can make drag estimates to pin down the maximum

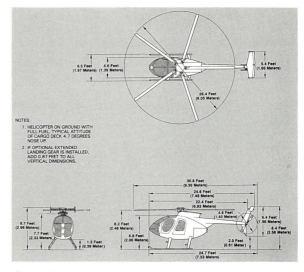

*General Arrangement Drawing*

speed and the mission fuel required. The remainder of the preliminary design process will be one of continuous changes in both gross weight and

## Key to Inboard Profile Drawing (facing page)

1. T-700-GE-701 Engine (Typical)
2. APU Drive Shaft
3. Integral Work Platform
4. Main Transmission Oil Coolers
5. Fire Detection Sensors (Typical)
6. Nacelle Door (Work Platform) (Typical)
7. Utility Pneumatic Connection
8. Ground Pneumatic Connection
9. Engine Support Frame (Typical)
10. Ammunition Bay
11. Rotor Control Mixer
12. Windshield Wipers
13. Ammunition Conveyor (Typical)
14. Forward Ground Service Panel
  A. Utility Light Receptacle
  B. Ground Power Receptacle
15. Retractable Searchlight
16. HELLFIRE Missile Cluster (Typical)
17. Landing Gear Fairing (Typical)
18. Articulated Rotor System
19. Antenna Spiral Radar Warning (AS2892/APR39)
20. RH Forward Avionics Bay (FAB)
  A. MUX Remote Terminal Unit Type I
  B. Gun Control Box
  C. Turret Control Box
  D. Fire Control Computer
  E. Remote HELLFIRE Electronic Unit
  F. Searchlight
  G. IHADSS Sight Electronic Unit (SEU)
  H. IHADSS Display Electronic Unit (DEU)
  J. PNVS Electronic Unit
  K. Fan
21. Electrical Power Center
  A. General Control Unit No. 1
  B. General Control Unit No. 2
  C. Protection Current Transformer
  D. Protection Current Transformer
  E. Loadmeter Current Transformer (T3)
  F. Loadmeter Current Transformer (T4)
  G. Generator Contactor No. 1
  H. Generator Contactor No. 2
  J. External Power Contactor
  K. Air Turbine Start Switch
  L. Tail Rotor Bus Tie Contactor Assembly
  M. Blade De-Ice Contactor
22. Turbine Speed Control Unit
23. SDC Particle Separator Inlet Duct
24. Hydraulic Oil Cooler
25. Auxiliary Power Unit (APU)
26. APU Fire Detector
27. Hydraulic Accumulator
28. Rate Gyro No. 2
29. APU Exhaust
30. Utility GSE Connection
31. Primary GSE Connection
32. Hydraulic Hand Pump
33. Utility Light Receptacle
34. Tail Rotor Drive Shaft

35. Drive Shaft Damper (Typical)
36. Chaff Dispenser
37. Static Discharge Wick (Typical)
38. 4-Bladed Tail Rotor Assembly
39. Tail Rotor Control Rod
40. Antiflail Unit (Typical)
41. Utility Manifold
42. LH Side Deck Area
  A. Doppler Navigation Set ASN/128
  B. Automatic Direction Finder Set R1496/ARN89B
  C. Radar Warning Set AN/APR 39(V)1
43. Stabilator Controller No. 1
44. ENCU Exhaust
45. Stabilator Controller No. 2
46. Infrared Suppressor Exhaust System
47. Rate Gyro No. 1
48. Environmental Control Unit (ENCU)
49. Wing
50. Ground Crew Intercom Receptacle (Typical)
51. Formation and Navigational Lights
  (1 each side RH and LH Wing)
52. Pitot/Static Sensor
53. Engine Nose Gearbox
54. Ice Detector Sensor
55. External Stores Control Unit
56. LH Forward Avionics Bay (FAB)
  A. TADS Electronic Unit
  B. Laser Electronic Unit
  C. MUX Remote Terminal Type I
  D. Multichannel Dimmer
  E. Radar Jammer
  F. Symbol Generator
  G. TADS Power Supply
  H. Data Communication Device
  J. Fan
57. Throttle Quadrant (Typical)
58. Antenna Spiral Radar Warning (AS2891/APR39)
59. Pilot's Night Vision Sensor (PNVS)
60. Optical Relay Tube
61. FM Homing Antennas (2)
62. Boresight Reticle Unit (BRU) (Typical)
63. Copilot/Gunner Armored Seat
64. IHADSS Integrated Helmet Unit (IHU)
65. IHADSS Helmet Display Unit (HDU) (Typical)
66. IHADSS Sensor Surveying Unit (SSU) (Typical)
67. Transparent, Ballistic Shield
68. Rollover Structure
69. Pilot Armored Seat, Extended Glare Shield
70. Main Rotor Actuators (3)
71. Stationary Swashplate
72. Pitch Control Link
73. Air Data Sensor
74. Rotating Swashplate
75. IR Jammer AN/ALQ 144(V)
76. AC Generator
77. Main Transmission
78. Rotor Support Structure
79. Transmission Driven Hydraulic Pump (2)
80. Tail Rotor Drive Shaft Disconnect Coupling

81. Intermediate Gearbox
82. Tail Rotor Gearbox
83. Removable Fairing
84. Tail Rotor Hydraulic Actuator
85. Antenna VHF AM/FM No. 1 (COMM) AN/ARC-186)
86. Tip Installation Assembly
  A. LH Antenna Spiral Radar Warning (AS2892/APR39)
  B. RH Antenna Spiral Radar Warning (AS2891/APR39)
  C. Navigational Tail Light, and Formation Light on Top of Vertical
87. Swiveling Tail Gear
88. Energy Absorbing Strut
89. Stabilator
90. Actuator/Stabilator
91. Tie Down/Jack Pad
92. Blade Antennas
93. Antenna ADF Loop (AS2108/ARN89B)
94. External Power Receptacle
95. Antenna Radar Altimeter XMTR (AS2595/APN194)
96. Survival Kit Bay
97. Doppler Radar Antenna
98. Antenna Radar Altimeter RCVR (AS2595/APN194)
99. Aft Avionic Bay (RH Side)
  A. Computer Kit 1A/TSEC ES-D-217493
  B. Battery Power Relay HS4200
  C. Battery Charger
  D. Filtre
  E. Communication Security KY28 TSEC/KY28
  F. Battery NI-CAD
  G. Video Recorder (Provisions)
  H. Aft Avionics Bay Fan
  J. AC External Power Monitor
  K. Data Link Termination Unit (2 Units)
  L. Air Data Processor
  M. HARS Unit
  N. Engine Turbine Speed Control
  O. Radar Altimeter RCVR/XMTR
  P. APU Circuit Breaker HS4844-5RO
  Q. Maintenance Light Circuit Breaker HS4844-5RO
  R. Module Electronic Assembly — M1309311431
100. Aft Storage Bay (LH Side)
  A. Kit, Tiedown, A/C Mooring (GFE)
  B. Tiedown Assembly, Main Rotor
  C. Pole Assembly, Main Rotor Blade Tiedown
  D. Pouch Stowage, Safety Pins
  E. Kit, Protective Covers A/C
101. Aft Fuel Tank
102. Gravity Fuel Filling Point
103. Rotor Brake
104. Ammunition Magazine (Flat Pack)
105. Nitrogen Inerting Unit
106. Single Point Refueling Manifold
107. Main Landing Gear
108. Energy Absorbing Main Landing Gear Strut
109. Forward Fuel Cell
110. Area Weapon Subsystem (AWS)
111. Flight Controls
112. Target Acquisition Designation Sight (TADS)

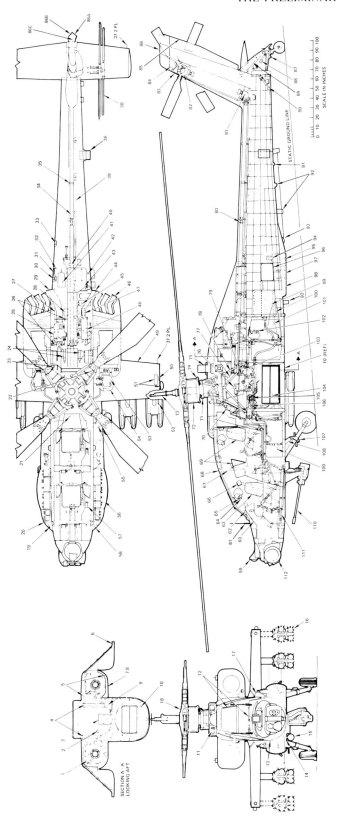

*Inboard Profile Drawing*

82-C10-1E   1-16-84

rotor diameter as more and more of the details are finalised allowing the weight engineers and aerodynamicists to make more and more precise estimates.

Other specialists will also contribute. Many of the preliminary design decisions will be influenced by the recommendations of those concerned with manufacturing, maintainability, reliability, cost, piloting, human factors, and operational suitability. In most projects, the preliminary design phase will gradually give way to the detail design phase in which drawings suitable for making parts will start to be generated. In other projects, the detail design will not be started until a 'go-ahead decision' can be made based on the economic projections for the new helicopter.

# Weight Management

An extra pound or kilogramme of empty weight on an aeroplane usually results in nothing more serious than a small increase in the take-off distance. An extra pound or kilogramme of empty weight on a helicopter, however, results in something very serious – a reduction in allowable payload. For this reason, the helicopter designer must take advantage of all possible weight saving methods while also never losing sight of his responsibility in the fields of safety, cost, reliability, maintainabilty, and crash worthiness.

A successful weight management programme involves the following features:

— High priority for low weight is established by the highest level of engineering management.
— Challenging weight goals (sometimes called 'bogies') are set for the designer of each component.
— Continual auditing of component weights, by weight engineers independent of the design

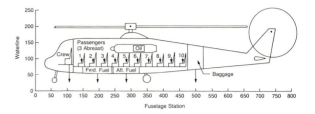

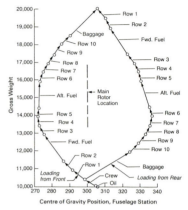

*The CG Diagram*

engineers, is maintained from preliminary design through production.

The weight engineers are also responsible for keeping track of the location of the centre of gravity and reporting if during the design process, it is being forced out of previously agreed ranges by decisions on the location of components. The graphical presentation of the centre of gravity location is the so-called 'c.g. potato' which shows the extreme locations as the useful load is loaded starting with either the most aft or the most forward elements.

The weight engineers will also compute the moments of inertia of the aircraft for use by the stability and control engineers and the dynamicists.

# The Other Configurations

At the beginning of the helicopter era, no one configuration was dominant. Assorted designers weighed differently the advantages and disadvantages of the various arrangements of rotors and types of power plants and as a result produced a wide variety of vertical-flight machines. With experience, many of the configurations lost their adherents for one reason or another. At this writing, with one exception, only the shaft-driven, main rotor-tail rotor type remains in production. It is not clear, however, that this is a permanent situation since the reasons for choosing this particular configuration over the others are that its advantages marginally exceed its disadvantages. In the future, a clever designer of one of the other configurations may be able to justify that his design is marginally better than the current king. It seems well therefore to describe the alternatives in order to prepare for their possible return. In another category are those configurations that combine the good vertical flight characteristics of the helicopter with the high speed capabilities of the aeroplane.

## Two-Rotor Systems

A single shaft-driven main rotor applies a torque to the fuselage that must be balanced with a force acting through a moment arm. A tail rotor or a small fan called a fenestron is the current way to produce this force. This configuration was not the obvious one to early helicopter designers. Almost all of them used a second main rotor to balance the effects of the first. Although these configurations have generally lost favour with modern designers, they do have some attractive features that might warrant reconsideration.

### Coaxial Helicopters

The most reasonable solution to the unbalanced torque problem in a shaft-driven helicopter is to turn one half of the rotor system in one direction and the other half in the other direction on the same axis of rotation. This rationale led most of the early helicopter pioneers to choose the coaxial design.

The coaxial configuration shares with the synchropter and the tandem the major advantage that it has no tail rotor absorbing 10 to 20 per cent of the engine power. Thus almost all of the output of the engine can be used to produce useful thrust and there is no need for the extra weight and complexity of a tail rotor nor concern about its danger.

Compared to helicopters with tail rotors, the coaxial configuration has everything desirable in a helicopter: efficient use of installed power, low structural weight, ground safety, and compactness (except, perhaps, vertically). The compactness undoubtedly is one reason why the Soviet Navy keeps the coaxial Kamov designs in production for shipboard operation.

Although the tail rotor is unnecessary for antitorque on these aircraft, it is sorely missed in its role as a source of directional, or yaw, control. The most common method of obtaining directional control on coaxials is to rig the pedals to increase the collective pitch on one rotor while reducing it on the other thus generating a difference in torque between the two rotors. If the gearing is right, the total rotor thrust will remain constant while the unbalanced torque will produce a yawing acceleration in the desired direction. Once the yaw rate is established, the pedals can be nearly neutralised, leaving only enough torque to overcome the fuselage aerodynamic damping.

The system works well in powered flight but not in autorotation, where it does not work at all or it works backward! One partial solution is to use one or more vertical surfaces with movable rudders to at least provide positive control when the aircraft has some forward velocity. Another solution was incorporated in the Gyrodyne DASH (Drone Anti-Submarine Helicopter), a remotely controlled torpedo carrier built for the

*(clockwise): designs from American engineers including Young, Sikorsky, and Hiller.*

US Navy. Movable drag vanes were installed on each blade tip of the two-bladed rotors and connected to the directional control system in such a way that when a turn was desired, the vanes on one rotor were deployed to increase its torque while leaving the vanes on the other rotor in their streamline position. Although producing positive directional control in all flight conditions, this concept has the disadvantage that even in their streamline positions, the vanes produce some drag resulting in a power penalty that the engine must overcome.

A variation of this scheme has been tried on some experimental prototypes by using brake shoes to engage either one or the other of the concentric shafts. This may be an eventual solution if mechanical reliability and fail-safe operation can be assured.

If, despite the directional-control problem, the designer elects to use the coaxial configuration to save on anti-torque power, he is handed one additional aerodynamic advantage and also one aerodynamic disadvantage. The advantage is found in the absence of swirl in the wake due to

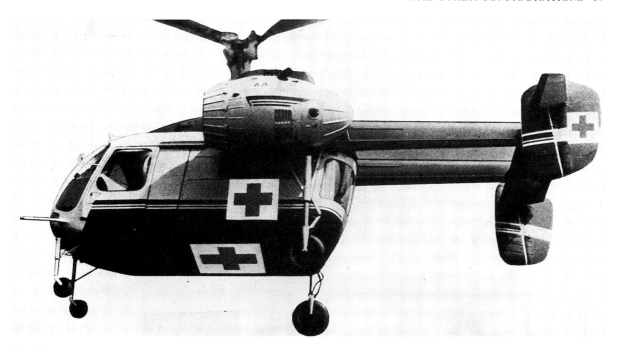

*The Kamov Ka-26 in the air ambulance configuration.*
**(Paul Beaver collection)**

the compensation of the lower rotor. A single rotor generates a wake with a swirl in the same direction as rotor rotation. The energy associated with this swirl represents a power loss. It is fairly small for rotors with relatively low disc loadings but becomes significant as disc loadings go above about 10 lb/ft$^2$ (2.05 kg/m$^2$) as modern trends seem to be taking them. The lower rotor of the coaxial configuration takes out most, if not all, the swirl put in by the upper rotor, thus eliminating the power loss.

The aerodynamic disadvantage exists if there is a significant separation between the upper and

**Lower Rotor Downwash Environment**

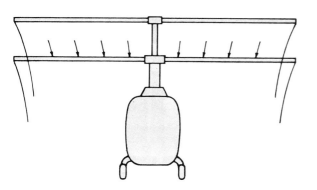

lower rotors. In this case the lower rotor operates in a perpetual 'climb' condition in the maturing wake of the upper rotor.

The further the two rotors are apart, the harder the lower rotor must work to develop its share of the thrust. Tests on a coaxial model with the rotors spaced about one-quarter radius apart showed that the penalty due to the lower rotor climb power just about cancelled out the power saving due to its anti-swirl contribution. In spacing the rotors, the designer must weigh the relatively minor results of this aerodynamic effect against the major – and disastrous – results of two limber hinged blades striking together in flight.

One way to minimise this potential problem is to use rigid, non-hinged blades as on the Sikorsky Advancing Blade Concept (ABC) aircraft.

The rigid blades on this aircraft came not as a deliberate result of an attempt to minimise the distance between rotors, but as a result of implementing a concept in which the limitations of retreating blade stall are eliminated by letting each rotor fly with asymmetrical lift with the advancing side highly loaded and the retreating side not. The resulting rolling moment in each rotor is carried to the shaft by the rigid blades where it is balanced by the other rotor. With this scheme, the ABC helicopter is able to fly faster than a normal helicopter by having only the advancing tip compressibility problem to contend

*Sikorsky's S-69 ABC Demonstrator with co-axial rotors.*

with; and that can be delayed until high forward speeds by designing and operating at low rotor tip speeds.

## Synchropter Helicopters

Like the coaxial, the synchropter has two closely-spaced rotors turning in opposite directions, but unlike the coaxial, which has both rotors on the same shaft, the synchropter has its rotors mounted on separate, but adjoining shafts at the same height above the fuselage. When they rotate, the rotors intermesh like an egg-beater. The configuration was invented by Anton Flettner in Germany just before the Second World War. The design team considered and rejected both main-rotor/tail-rotor and tandem configurations as being too complex before choosing the synchropter. Flettner's FL-282 was the world's first production helicopter, preceding Igor Sikorsky's R-4 by several months. A total of 24 Fl-282's were delivered before Allied bombers destroyed the factory.

Note that at least on small synchropters such as this one, the absence of the tail rotor does not eliminate the danger to ground personnel working around the aircraft when the rotors are turning.

The synchropter configuration was also adopted in the US by Kellett who built two experimental prototypes, the XR-8 which first flew in 1944 and the twin-engine XR-10 which flew three years later. Neither of the Kellett synchropters entered production but later the Kaman Aircraft Company built several hundred synchropters for the US military services.

The synchropter shares with the coaxial the efficient use of engine power and compactness allowed by the absence of the tail rotor. It is even more compact than the coaxial since the two rotors are at the same height rather than being one above the other on the same shaft. Blade clearance is achieved by careful synchronisation rather than by vertical displacement.

Along with the advantages, the synchopter also shares the coaxial's disadvantage of uncertain directional control; especially in autorotation since yaw control is primarily obtained with differential torque induced by differential collective pitch. For this reason, they are equipped with vertical stabilisers and rudders to help with directional control when there is some forward speed. Kaman also used differential lateral cyclic pitch to help produce a yawing moment and a reversal of the directional control when the collective lever was down in the autorotational position to compensate for the reversal produced by aerodynamic effects in this mode of flight.

Another problem for the synchropter is the difficulty in using more than two blades on each rotor because of blade strike problems. This was one of the major reasons that the three-bladed Kellet synchropters were not successful.

## Tandem Helicopters

The other logical two-rotor configuration is the tandem. Its capability for positive yaw control is greater than that of the coaxial or syncropter because its two rotors are located at a reasonable distance from the centre of gravity. Yaw control is obtained with differential lateral cyclic pitch operated by the rudder pedals. The resultant opposite tilt of the rotor thrust vectors produces a yawing moment about the centre of gravity.

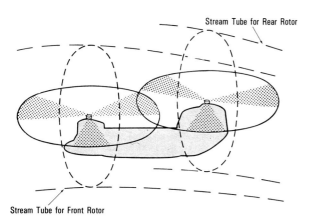

*Overlapping of Affected Stream Tubes*

*Boeing Chinook HC Mk1, UK Royal Air Force.*

Longitudinal control is achieved by using fore-and-aft motion of the control stick to produce differential collective pitch that changes the relative thrust of the two rotors. On most modern tandem helicopters, a trim control for longitudinal cyclic pitch adjusts the tilt of the tip path planes to reduce rotor flapping. This ensures adequate fuselage-blade clearance and minimises the oscillatory forces coming from the rotor hubs.

Roll control by sidewise motion of the stick is exactly the same as it is for main-rotor/tail-rotor configurations: lateral cyclic pitch tilts the two tip path planes in the same direction thus producing a rolling moment about the centre of gravity.

The tandem configuration is a natural for handling large centre of gravity shifts that might occur during loading since with differential collective pitch, the two rotors can be developing different thrusts. This is a definite advantage over the single rotor configuration which by its very nature is limited to the amount of offset centre of gravity it can easily handle.

The tandem's lifting capability is superior to that of the single rotor configuration because almost all of the engine power can go to the rotors instead of ten to twenty per cent of it being used to accomplish the anti-torque task. Since all rotors use about the same tip speed, the smaller diameter rotors of the tandem turn at higher rpm. This results in less speed reduction between the engine and the rotors and less torque in the drive system. Both effects tend to reduce the total drive system weight compared to the single rotor configuration with tail rotor.

Up against these advantages are some less advantageous factors. All streamline fuselages are directionally unstable. If allowed to find their own way through the air, they would all turn broadside. A tail rotor is an effective stabilising device and can be easily augmented with fixed vertical stabilisers. On a tandem, however, the short moment arm available between the centre of gravity and the aft end of the fuselage makes it difficult to achieve good directional stability even with a large aft pylon or extra vertical surfaces. It has been found necessary on high-speed tandems to artificially augment directional stabilty with automatic control systems that sense sideslip angle and use differential lateral cyclic pitch to minimise it.

In some flight situations, the lack of strong directional stability is an 'enhancing' characteristic of the tandem since it makes it relatively insensitive to wind direction while landing on a ship or manoeuvring close to obstacles in a gusty wind.

Flying one rotor behind the other in forward flight has a couple of disadvantages. First, the rotors are working on the same relatively small

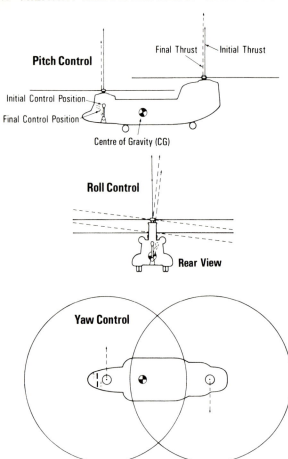

**Pitch Control**

Final Thrust   Initial Thrust

Initial Control Position

Final Control Position

Centre of Gravity (CG)

**Roll Control**

**Rear View**

**Yaw Control**

*Tandem Rotor Helicopter Controls*

air mass and must therefore impart more total energy to produce lift.

This shows up as increased induced power. A tandem in sideward flight, on the other hand, works with a larger air mass than a single rotor helicopter and as a consequence requires less power. This can be used to improve low speed performance by flying sideways.

The other disadvantage has to do with longitudinal stabilty. To obtain a stable nose-down pitching moment when the angle of attack of the helicopter increases due to an up-gust, the rear rotor must increase its thrust more than the front rotor. This is difficult to achieve because the rear rotor, acting in the increasing downwash of the front rotor, does not experience as much thrust increase as it would in clean air. This situation is especially aggravated if the centre of gravity position is aft of the midpoint such that the front rotor has a larger moment arm than the aft. For

this reason, the unlimited centre of gravity capability of the tandem that allows it to handle various loadings in hover is compromised when the helicopter must fly forwards. An aft limit must be set and observed even with an automatic stability augmentation system. Comparing the advantanges and disadvantages of the tandem configuration against the main-rotor/tail-rotor configuration has been the object of many design studies.

The general conclusion is that the single rotor design is more attractive for small helicopters (those below about 20000 lbs (9072 kg)) but as helicopters get larger, the tandem is more and more competitive. The fact of the matter is, however, that at the time of this writing there are no new tandem rotor helicopters being developed for production and the largest helicopters flying are of the single rotor configuration.

## Side-By-Side Helicopters

The advantage that the tandem has in sidewards flight, the side-by-side has in forward flight. The two rotors working on a large stream tube of air account for less induced power than a single rotor helicopter just as the induced drag of an airplane is reduced by increasing its wingspan. This was probably not the prime motivation in developing the first of the modern, successful helicopters, the side-by-side Focke Wulf Fw-61. The motivation for the configuratiion decision on that aircraft was probably one of minimising the structural changes when converting a rather conventional aeroplane into a helicopter.

*Focke-Achgelis Fa 61.*

*Bell XV-15 tilt-rotor demonstrator*

The side-by-side configuration has the disadvantage that the structure is used rather inefficiently, and the difficulty of obtaining a satisfactory solution to the dynamic problem of the highly loaded wing support structure is formidable. Despite this, several helicopters of this design reached the prototype stage and one, the Fa 223, went into production in Germany during the final months of the Second World War, but only nine had been completed before the Soviet Army overran the factory.

The configuration, of course, is also used as the basis for the tilt rotor aircraft that combines the low speed features of the helicopter with the high speed features of the aeroplane.

# Multi-Rotored Helicopters

Some designers have been intrigued by the idea of using three or four or more rotors to support the helicopter in order to take advantage of the low weight of small, fast-turning rotors and a simple control system needing only collective pitch to each rotor. Several such helicopters have

reached the prototype stage but none have as yet advanced into production.

# Helicopters with Jet-Powered Rotors

## Ram and Pulse Jet Systems

If a driving force can be applied to the rotor blades themselves rather than to the rotor shaft, there is no torque reaction on the fuselage and so neither an anti-torque device nor a heavy transmission is needed. Thus a very simple helicopter with a high payload-to-gross weight ratio can be designed. The first attempts at this type of propulsion scheme used motor-driven propellers mounted on the blades. None of these succeeded, probably because of the very hostile dynamic environment for the motors and propellers. It was with great enthusiasm, then, that helicopter designers welcomed the ram-jet and the pulse-jet that had been developed in Germany during the Second World War for use on missiles and aeroplanes. Here were two rugged propulsion systems with either no moving parts or just a few that operated best in the high sub-sonic speed regime right where a helicopter blade tip operated. Both were soon flying on a number of promising helicopter test-beds.

*Convertiwings (above) and Cierva Workhorse (below)*
*are examples of multi-rotored prototypes*

Only one of these, the ram-jet powered Dutch Kolibri, was produced in quantity and that production run resulted in only 25 aircraft. All of these jet-powered helicopters had two basic operational problems: they were very fuel-inefficient and they were terribly noisy. Their developers had an answer for each objection: 'These jets will burn anything and so fuel will always be cheap; and people get used to noisy machines.' It is really not necessary to point out how wrong they were.

Although a tip-powered helicopter needs no tail rotor for anti-torque, it does need something for directional control. Several of the designers originally tried to use a rudder whose hinge line was tilted so that the surface could produce a

*McDonnell's Little Henry (above) which tested ram-jet concepts and the Kolibri (below).*

*Hiller Hornet design (above) and American Helicopters XH-26 Jet Jeep of 1952 (below).*

force both in hover using the rotor downwash and in forward flight. The flight condition in which this scheme does not work well is in the landing flare following a descent. In this manoeuvre, the rotor wake may not envelop the rudder and the forward speed may be too low to produce a significant force. Several accidents occurred when helicopters rolled over after touching down with some sideward motion which the pilots were unable to correct. (This was also a frequent cause of accidents on autogiros.) As a result of these accidents, most of the tip-jet powered developments ended up with small tail rotors that gave positive directional control in all flight conditions.

The revival of the tip-jet powered configuration for military purposes would probably only be viable for very large helicopters using more efficient turbo-jet engines and then only for those missions where the advantages of its simplicity and high payload-to-gross weight ratio would overcome its operational disadvantages of poor fuel economy and high noise. Certainly one modern consideration would be the high visibility such helicopters would have to heat-seeking missiles.

## Pressure-Jet Helicopters

Second World War Austria was the home of another type of rotor-driven helicopter. This was the pressure-jet configuration in which air was supplied to the rotor hub from an air compressor in the fuselage and then ducted out the hollow blades to nozzles at the tip where it was turned and ejected like water from a lawn sprinkler. The first of these was the Doblhoff Wn 342.

*The Doblhoff Wn 342, later captured by the US Army.*

The air compressor on this helicopter did not produce enough pressure to hover the machine so fuel was mixed with the air and burned in the blade-tip nozzels to provide an after-burner effect. The Wn 342 was developed too late to reach production in Germany, but following the war, members of its scattered design team were instrumental in building several helicopters based on the same principle; in the United Kingdom with the Fairey Rotordyne and Ultra Light, in France with the SNCASO Ariel and Farfadet, and in the USA with the Hughes XH-17 and the McDonnell XV-1. All of these used tip burning and as a consequence were very noisy.

*Howard Hughes' XH-17 heavy-lift helicopter of 1952 (above) Fairey Rotordyne, (below) which first flew in November 1957. McDonnell XV-1 convertiplane (bottom)*

*Sud-Ouest/Djinn, a two-seat utility helicopter which served the French Army 1956–1966.*

because the gasses in the blades are at about 1300°F (704°C). This system was used on the Hughes XV-9 demonstrator that was built as a proof-of-concept aircraft on which a much larger flying crane helicopter could be based.

A more efficient version of the pressure-jet would use a turbofan instead of a jet engine to feed the rotor. For this 'warm cycle' vehicle, the blade temperature would be about 800°F (426°C).

The main attraction of any of the tip-jet powered configurations is that as shaft-driven helicopters grow in size, the transmissions become very heavy because of the large speed reduction from the engine to the rotor and because of the large torques associated with the low rotor speeds. According to theory, the transmission weight should go up as the cube of the rotor diameter while the lifting capability of the rotor is increasing only by the square. Thus a design that has no transmission should have a definite advantage when especially large helicopters are considered. At one time, it was thought that the difference would give the pressure-jet an unbeatable advantage for helicopters as small as 10 000 lbs (4536 kg), but the successful development of single rotor, shaft-driven helicopters above 100 000 lbs (45 360 kg) has effectively raised the break-even weight. In addition, the possibility of lifting large loads with two or more helicopters working together has reduced the

To solve the noise problem, a 'cold' pressure jet was developed in France as the Sud-Ouest Djinn. Its air compressor was large enough that no fuel needed to be burned at the blade tips and as a consequence, the Djinn was quiet, although still not as fuel-efficient as a shaft driven helicopter. Almost 200 of these were built, primarily for use by the French Army.

The 'cold' in the description of the Djinn propulsion system, is only relative since the air heats up to about 300°F (148°C) as it is being compressed. One of the fallouts of this system is the very good anti-icing characteristics of the hot blades.

There is also a 'hot' system in which the exhaust gasses from a jet engine are ducted to the blades. In this case, there is a design problem

*Hughes XV-9 hot-cycle propulsion test bed.*

motivation to develop those large helicopters for which the pressure-jet might be the only logical choice.

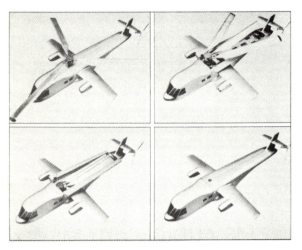

*The Bell Research Compound Helicopter*

# Helicopters that go Fast

The 'pure' helicopter is limited to about 200 kts (370 km/h) by a combination of compressibility effects on the advancing blade and stall effects on the retreating blade. If a new aircraft is required to go faster than 200 kts and still retain the good hover capability of the helicopter, other configurations must be considered. These include compound helicopters with a wing and a propulsive device, tilt rotor aircraft, or aircraft on which the rotor can be stopped and either stowed or used as a non-rotating wing.

## Compound Helicopters

These aircraft may be considered to be aeroplanes which have an effective low-speed lifting device. They use a wing and some form of auxiliary propulsion such as propellers, ducted fans, or jet engines to relieve the rotor of all, or nearly all, of its lifting and propulsive duties at high speeds. This eliminates the retreating blade stall problem and if the rotor is slowed, it can delay the advancing blade compressibility problem as well. This configuration is probably the best choice for speeds up to about 300 kts (555 km/h). A Bell UH-1 with a wing and two jet engines flew to 274 kts (507 km/h) in the mid 1960s.

Jet engines are convenient for research projects since they can be quickly added without interfering with the existing power train but they are fuel-inefficient at speeds where these aircraft are likely to fly so a better propulsion device is the variable pitch propeller as was used on the Lockheed AH-56 Cheyenne.

The propeller, besides providing the means to fly fast, has other attributes valuable for combat helicopters. It can be used to change the aircraft's pitch attitude at any speed. In hover, for instance, this type of helicopter can be held either nose-up or nose-down to increase its

*Lockheed AH-56A Cheyenne rigid-rotor design.*

usuable field of fire. Another use is as a speed brake in forward flight. This is valuable when precise decelerations and descents are required.

The propeller can also be used to accelerate the aircraft from hover without the need to tilt the fuselage. This might be of some value in minimising the exposure in nap-of-the-earth flying but it has its limitations. The propeller on the AH-56 could develop about 2000 lbs (907 kg) of static thrust. This resulted in a forward acceleration of just over 0.1G compared to nearly 1.0G if cyclic pitch were used to tilt the entire aircraft nose-down.

The power to operate the propulsive devices depends on their power loading: the ratio of thrust to horsepower. For propellers and ducted fans, this ratio is primarily a function of their diameter; the bigger the better.

Any one of these systems, while helping performance at high speed, reduces it in hover because its weight comes out of the payload capability and because in some systems it draws power while 'idling' that could have been used by the main rotor.

## Tilt Rotor Aircraft

By mounting the rotors on the wing tips and providing the mechanism to convert them into

*The first V-22 Osprey at its public debut in May 1988.*
*(Paul Beaver)*

propellers, the limitation on maximum speed capability is increased above what is feasible for the compound helicopter. Theoretically, a tilt rotor aircraft should be able to fly as fast as any other propeller-driven aeroplane – more than 400 kts (740 km/h) – if it has enough power. The Bell/Boeing V-22 Osprey is expected to have a maximum speed of about 350 kts (648 km/h).

Because of the high power required to go fast, the designers of these aircraft can afford to use relatively high disc loadings in hover. This minimises the size and weight of the aircraft but at the same time produces high downwash velocities in hover which might make operations from unprepared sites difficult because of ground erosion.

## Stopped Rotor Aircraft

Even when working as a propeller on a tilt-rotor aircraft, the rotor runs into aerodynamic limits due to compressibility. For speeds above about 400 kts (740 km/h), the designer will probably want to consider stopping the rotor and either stowing it or using it as a wing. The stowed-rotor concept was proposed by Lockheed when the US Army was interested in such aircraft in the late 1960s and the rotor/wing concept is embodied in the X-Wing.

Whether stopping a rotor to fold it or to make it into a wing, some rather formidible technical problems must be overcome. When a rotor is

turning at full speed, the blades are so stiffened by centrifugal forces that aerodynamic loads cannot bend them significantly. Compensating for the loss of centrifugal stiffening during the stopping process is the primary engineering challenge for designers of these aircraft.

It is especially critical when the rotor is moving slowly through the forward-left quadrant where it is acting as a swept-forward wing going backward through the air. Here it is subject to aeroelastic instability both in bending and in twisting unless the designer has given it large bending and torsional stiffnesses.

# The Main Rotor

Many detailed decisions concerning the rotors and the stabilising surfaces need to be made before the design is complete. The most sophisticated of the computer preliminary design programs contain logical procedures for making some, but not all of these. Many have to be based on considerations that are impossible to computerise and depend on factors ranging from solid scientific fact to controversial aesthetic judgement. In almost all cases, there are powerful arguments pulling the designer in opposite directions. Resolving these dilemmas so as to achieve the 'least worst compromise' is the designer's primary task.

## Main Rotor Parameters

### Diameter

— Should be large for good hover and vertical climb performance.
— Should be small for low total aircraft weight and cost, ease of storage, and flying between closely-spaced trees in the nap-of-the-earth.

The designer's goal is to find the smallest diameter which will produce the required performance without violating other constraints that experience has established. The customer may have set an upper limit on the disc loading since high values can give operational problems when flying close to unprepared surfaces as the strong downwash 'placer mines' the ground filling the air with earth, gravel, and bushes. A disc loading of about 10 lb/ft$^2$ (2.05 kg/m$^2$) is generally considered to be the upper limit for operation over loosely compacted sites. On the other hand, certain operational requirements may force the designer to a higher disc loading to provide a small, compact aircraft which can successfully fit in existing hangars on small ships, negotiate the elevators and hangar decks of aircraft carriers, or fit in the cargo compartments of transport aircraft.

Another consideration is that high disc loadings result in high rates of descent in autorotation. The ability to autorotate is recognised as one of the inherent and desirable features of helicopters. Good autorotative capability is extremely important for single-engine helicopters since it is practiced extensively during pilot training, but even multi-engine helicopters are required to demonstrate full power-off autorotations and landings by both military and civil certificating authorities. Any rotor will autorotate if the rate of descent is high enough and, in theory at least, a successful landing can be made from any rate of descent if the stored energy in the rotor is sufficient. In practice, however, the pilot's chances of making a good landing from high rates of descent are limited by his reaction time and his ability to judge the precise altitude at which to initiate the landing flare. Tests on aeroplanes have shown that satisfactory deadstick landings can be consistently made by average pilots if the steady rate of descent is less than about 2500 ft/min (7625 m/sec), but that at higher rates, increased pilot skills are required. Although similar tests have not been done on helicopters, experience with some experimental ramjet-powered helicopters (with poor autorotational characteristics because of the drag of their jets) seems to verify that 2500 ft/min is a reasonable upper limit that should at least apply to single-engine helicopters for which the risk of engine failure is relatively high. Whether that limit should also apply to multi-engine helicopters is still a subject for debate.

### Tip Speed

— Should be high for low rotor and drive system weight and for a good aerodynamic environment on the retreating side in forward flight.
— Should be low for low noise and for a good aerodynamic environment on the advancing side in forward flight.

The designer's goal is to pick the highest tip speed he can within certain constraints; one of which is noise. It is generally agreed today that tip speeds of more than about 775 ft/sec (236 m/s) are unacceptably noisy and that tip speeds of less than 500 ft/sec (152 m/s) are 'quiet'. The first Bell UH-1 was designed with a rotor diameter of 44 ft (13.4 m) and a tip speed of 740 ft/sec (225 m/s). Later versions, such as the UH-1H, used a 48 ft (14.6 m) diameter rotor and the same rpm so that the tip speed was well over 800 ft/sec (244 m/s). This partially accounts for the high noise signature of these particular helicopters. Later Bell designs, such as the Models 206 and 222 are much quieter, having tip speeds in the region of 760 ft/sec (232 m/s). The quietest recent helicopter was the experimental Hughes 'Quiet One', a specially modified OH-6, with a tip speed of only 430 ft/sec (131 m/sec).

A lower overall limit on tip speed is set by the requirement to store energy in the rotor in case of an engine failure.

Avoiding advancing tip compressibility and retreating tip stall in forward flight also limits the choices of rotor speed. It is generally accepted that for straight blades, advancing tip Mach numbers of more than about 0.92 will produce high loads in the blades and control system due to 'Mach tuck', the sudden nose-down pitching moment generated as shock waves form on the airfoil. Sweeping the tip can increase the critical Mach number by several per cent but with the penalty of increased manufacturing cost.

It is also generally accepted that retreating blade stall is unavoidable on conventional helicopters at tip speed ratios (forward speed divided by tip speed) of more than about 0.5. The figure below shows how these constraints limit the available choices of design tip speed as the forward speed goal is increased. It also shows why the maximum speed of 'pure' helicopters is around 200 kts (370 km/h).

## Blade Area

— Should be small (but not too small) for good hover performance as well as low blade weight and cost.
— Should be large for good manoeuvrability in forward flight.

Just as an aeroplane wing has an optimum angle of attack for its maximum lift-to-drag ratio, a rotor has an optimum angle of attack for its blade elements to achieve the maximum hover

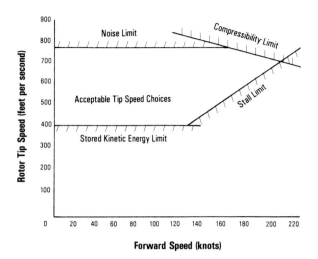

*Constraints on Choice of Tip Speeds*

performance. If the blade area is too high, the average angle of attack will be less than optimum and the hover performance will be worse than it might be. Yet, if a rotor were designed only for hover, it would probably have too little blade area to do the required high-G manoeuvres in forward flight without excessive blade stall. The basis for the design decision with regard to blade area was discussed earlier in the review of Helicopter Aerodynamics.

## Number of Blades

— Should be small for low cost, low hub drag, low hub weight, low vulnerability to combat damage, high torsional blade stiffness, and ease of storage.
— Should be high for low vibration, for ease of handling individual blades, and for less distinctive noise and visual signatures.

As can be seen from this list and from the variety used on existing helicopters, once the blade area has been selected, dividing it up into a certain number of blades is usually governed by considerations other than performance; but performance may be slightly influenced by the choice.

One of the small, but well documented, detrimental effects to hover performance is 'vortex interaction'. This arises when the tip of one blade comes close to the tip vortex left by a preceding blade. The locally induced change of angle of attack may produce a small region of stall with a resultant drag penalty. When the number of blades is small, the tip vortex from one blade is displaced further down in the wake before the next blade comes by and the potential for this problem is reduced.

Also, the smaller the number of blades used to achieve the required blade area the larger the chord. This is beneficial from a 'Reynolds number' standpoint. (Reynolds number is proportional to the product of the chord and the velocity). Higher Reynolds numbers result in slightly lower drag coefficients and higher maximum lift coefficients in the range of typical rotor blades. Penalties associated with low Reynolds numbers become significant if the blade chord is less than about 5 ins (13 cm).

There may be an aerodynamic penalty however, in using just a few blades to match the required blade area. If the blades come out too stubby – with radius-to-chord ratios of less than about eight – tip losses will probably be high enough to nullify the aforementioned advantages. On the other hand, ratios of above 12 or 13 make such a limber blade easy to bend and twist into odd shapes in flight.

In forward flight, a rotor with a large number of blades generates a smoother wake than does one with fewer blades. As a result, the induced power is expected to be somewhat less.

All of these performance advantages and disadvantages based on the number of blades are relatively small and generally are not 'decision drivers' compared to the items listed at the beginning of this section. Most modern design teams prefer to use four blades as a compromise between too few and too many but in some cases, a different number is chosen. For example, five blades are installed on the McDonnell Douglas 500D and subsequent models so they can use the same blade design developed for the lighter, four-blade 500C. The same reasoning accounts for Sikorsky going from six to seven blades when developing the CH-53E Super Stallion from earlier versions of the same aircraft, such as the CH-53A Sea Stallion.

## Twist

— Should be high for good hover performance and delay of retreating blade stall.
— Should be low for low vibration and blade loads in forward flight.

The rotor's hover performance is best when the induced velocity generated in the process of developing upward rotor thrust is uniform across the disc. For untwisted blades, the induced velocities are high outboard and low inboard. By twisting the blades to reduce the lift at the tip, the flow pattern can be made more uniform and the hover Figure of Merit can be improved by up to about 5 per cent. Since this may represent a 20 per cent increase in payload and since twisted blades are as easy to manufacture as untwisted blades, there is a good reason to use twist, and all modern helicopters do.

A study of the aerodynamics of hover shows that there is a non-linear 'ideal twist' that would theoretically even up the induced velocity distribution perfectly. At the centre of rotation the blade would be pointing straight up. Going outboard, the pitch would decrease at a decreasing rate out to the tip. For simplicity in manufacturing, most designers choose not to use this non-linear ideal twist. Instead, they choose a linear twist in which the blade is twisted nose-down at a constant rate in terms of degrees per foot from the blade attachment point to the tip. This nose-down twist is assigned a negative sign as shown below on the figure that illustrates the benefit in Figure of Merit that can be achieved with twist.

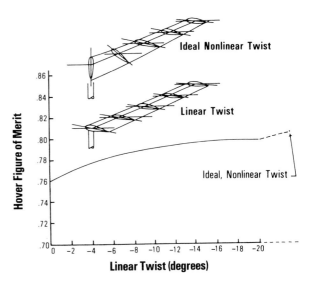

*Effect of Twist on Rotor Figure of Merit*

It may be seen that −20° of linear twist gives almost the same benefit as non-linear ideal twist and that most of the benefit comes in the first 10 or 12 degrees.

A variation on linear twist distribution is used on the Sikorsky UH-60A Black Hawk. Because the proximity of a blade tip vortex shed by the preceding blade causes a non-uniform angle of attack distribution on the following blade, the designers chose to use a compensating non-uniform twist distribution as shown below.

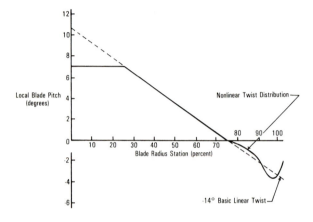

**Black Hawk Twist Modification**

While good in hover, high twist is bad in forward flight. This is due to the oscillating spanwise travel of the centre of lift as the blade goes around the azimuth with the lift being concentrated inboard on the advancing blade and outboard on the retreating. As the lift shifts back and forth, the blade bends in response resulting in oscillating forces at the rotor hub that produce vibration in the rest of the helicopter. The higher the twist, the higher these oscillating forces.

Not only does excessive twist cause vibration, but a performance penalty at high speeds as well. This is due to the negative angle of attack on the advancing tip that produces a download, thus nullifying the purpose of that part of the rotor. Even a moderate twist of $-10°$ produces this effect as a plot of local angle of attack shows.

There are two other considerations with regard to twist that should be mentioned: for an autogiro, the optimum twist is with the pitch at the tip more than at the root – just opposite to that of a helicopter; and for hover in ground effect, as would be necessary for a man-powered helicopter, the twist should be much lower than for hovering out of ground effect.

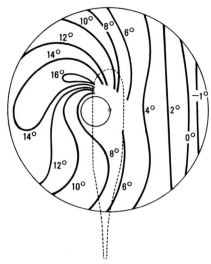

*Angle of Attack Distribution*

## Taper

— Should be zero for minimum cost to design and build.
— Should be high for good hover performance.
— May be unusual for good forward flight performance.

Blade twist can be used to give an uniform induced velocity distribution in hover, but on a constant-chord blade even ideal twist will result in a variation of the local angle of attack along the blade. Since an airfoil has one angle of attack at which its lift-to-drag ratio is a maximum, such variations are to be avoided. This can be done by combining ideal taper with ideal twist. It is theoretically possible to obtain another 2 per cent or 3 per cent increase in the Figure of Merit using this technique. Unfortunately, the ideal blade shape is one that is not very practical as shown below.

But fortunately, it is the outer half of the blade that is most important, so designers can obtain most of the benefit by using a constant chord out to some point and then using straight taper. To ensure that the blade area is sufficient, a simple rule-of-thumb is that the chord at the 75 per cent radius should be the same as it would be for a constant chord blade. A more rigorous method involves using the same 'thrust-weighted solidity'. Because of the detrimental effects of increasing skin friction drag coefficient and decreasing maximum lift coefficient that go along with low Reynolds numbers, taper may be counter-productive if the blade chord at the tip

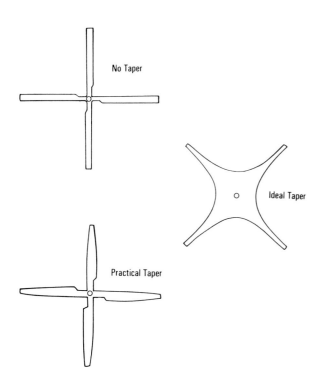

**Blade Taper Configurations**

*BERP Blade Configuration on a Westland Lynx.*

comes out to be less than about five inches. An additional consideration for small-chord tips is the potential difficulty of installing tip weights that might be required to tailor the blade dynamics or to ensure satisfactory autorotation entry and flare characteristics.

In spite of the fact that hover performance may be improved with a taper that results in a smaller chord at the tip than at the root, there is some evidence that inverse taper, with the tip chord larger than the root, has a place in the designer's list of options. From an intuitive standpoint, it is obvious that the outboard portions of the blades with their higher velocities are doing most of the work so for best use of blade weight, it would not be surprising to find that the optimum configuration would be with most of the blade area located near the tip. A rotor design that seems to be based on this principle is the one developed under the British Experimental Rotor Programme (BERP).

As a matter of fact, this design did not come about with the object of saving blade weight. It was an attempt to improve the aerodynamics of an existing blade by adding chord to achieve both leading edge sweep and a thinner airfoil to delay the Mach number at which compressibility effects became important. As a fallout, the stall angle of the retreating tip was also increased through the action of a vortex generated at the 'notch' which keeps the flow attached on the rest of the tip. This rotor, installed on a Westland Lynx, set the world absolute speed record for helicopters at 216 kts (342 km/h) in 1986. It is also used on the EH 101.

## Tip Shape

— Should be square for minimum cost to design, test, and build.
— Should be non-square to delay compressibility effects, reduce noise, and to introduce favourable dynamic aeroelastic twist.

The aerodynamics at the tip of an airplane wing in steady, straight flight are complicated enough, but not nearly so complex as the aerodynamics at the tip of a helicopter blade which is subjected to rapidly varying conditions. Besides the BERP tip, a number of others have been tried in experimental flight testing, but only a few have

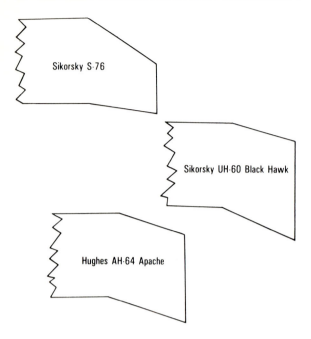

*Main-Rotor Tips*

shown enough advantage over straight tips to be incorporated in production designs. The figure shows tips that have been used both on experimental and on production helicopters.

In several of these cases, the leading edge has been swept back to delay the start of compressibility effects since it is only the component of velocity perpendicular to the leading edge that is governing.

As with most concepts in helicopter aerodynamics, this one is not as straight-forward as it might seem. Theory and experiments both show a lag in compressibility effects such that they peak after the blade enters the front half of the disc. This is where the straight blade naturally takes on a swept characteristic from the combination of rotational and forward speed; whereas the swept-back tip is being aerodynamically unswept and, in some circumstances, might suffer more than the straight tip. Flight experience with present swept-back tips seems to indicate, however, that compared to straight blades, they have gained more than they have lost in that their performance is improved through delaying the Mach tuck problem to a higher forward speed.

There has been some speculation that non-square tips might spread out the tip vortices and thus alleviate some of the problems of vortex interference both in hover and in forward flight where it leads to the impulse noise known as

'blade slap' during turns and slow descents. So far this is only speculation with no experimental results to make it into fact.

The highly swept tips of the Black Hawk and the Apache have a beneficial effect by producing 'dynamic twist' in forward flight. The download on the advancing tip acting behind the structural axis tends to twist the blade nose-up while the upload on the retreating tip tends to twist it nose-down. Both effects are beneficial in alleviating the normally unbalanced air loading distribution in forward flight. The effect also works in hover where the upload increases the twist thereby increasing the hover Figure of Merit. This blade tip configuration also has a beneficial fallout for flying qualities, since it improves speed stability. If the helicopter starts an uncommanded increase in speed, the advancing tip with its download will twist up causing the rotor to flap up in front pitching the helicopter nose-up and tending to return it to its original trim speed.

Unfortunately, nothing comes free. Swept tips complicate the structural design of the blade and doubly so if they must be replaceable in the field when damaged. These tips significantly increase the cost of designing, testing, and building.

## Root Cutout

— Should be low to minimise the drag on the advancing side.
— Should be high to minimise the drag and the download on the retreating side.

An airfoil shape can only be maintained inboard on the blade until it has to be replaced by whatever structural shape is necessary to attach the blade to the hub. Running the airfoil in as far as possible is beneficial on the advancing blade in forward flight and in hover because it streamlines the spar to minimise the drag. On the other hand, as shown below, the combination of high collective and high cyclic pitch required to trim the helicopter at high speeds means that the trailing edge of the blade in the reverse flow region is acting like a scoop shovel creating a large download and a high drag. Here it would be desirable to use a large cutout by starting the blade outboard of the reverse flow region.

Without some exotic mechanical or aerodynamic device, the designer cannot have it both ways. There is, however, a partial solution that Sikorsky used on the S-76. It is the untwisting of

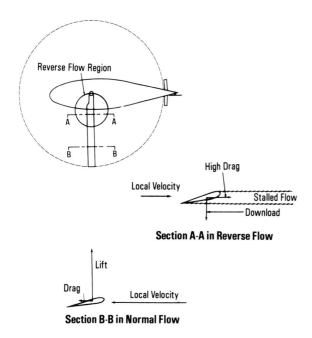

**Section A-A in Reverse Flow**

**Section B-B in Normal Flow**

*Conditions on the Retreating Blade*

the blade near its root as illustrated below. This decreases the negative angle of attack in the reversed flow region while not hurting too much on the advancing side.

## Rotor Inertia

— Should be high for good autorotative entry and flare characteristics.

— Should be low for minimum blade and hub weight.

Unlike most of the other parameters, the level of rotor inertia can not be seen during a walk-around inspection. It will be evident, however,

*Inboard Twist Modification*

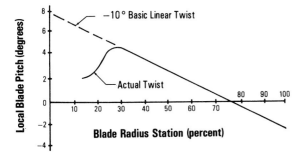

during the first practice autorotation. With too little inertia, the rotor speed will decay to a dangerous level after the power is chopped before the pilot can react by dropping collective pitch. If he does manage to survive the entry and get into steady autorotation, the landing flare will be cut short by low rpm as he raises the collective to halt his downward progress.

A rule-of-thumb for the rotor designer is that the kinetic energy stored in the rotor of a single-engine helicopter at normal rpm can supply the power required to hover for at least 1.5 sec before the rotor speed decays to the point that the blades stall. One and a half seconds does not sound like much, but tests have shown that it gives an adequate margin for average pilots.

This requirement usually means that weights must be installed in the blade tips. Whether the requirement of 1.5 sec must also apply to multi-engined helicopters is not clear; the argument hinging on how often a given helicopter will suffer, or have to demonstrate, a complete power failure.

## Direction of Rotation

— Should have the advancing blade on the right to make it consistent with previous US helicopters.

— Should have the advancing blade on the left to make it consistent with previous French and Soviet helicopters.

Since many pilots have successfully learned to fly helicopters with both types of rotation, there seems to be little logical reason to choose one over the other. The goal of the designer should be to pick the direction of rotation that results in the simplest and lightest drive-train between the engine and the rotor.

## Hinge Offset

— Should be low for small hub drag.

— Should be high for crisp manoeuvring in all flight conditions.

Flapping hinges can either be on the axis of rotation or offset from it. Most of the autogiros and many early helicopters had zero offset. Designers of current multi-bladed rotors now offset the hinges while designers of two-bladed rotors have stayed with the zero offset or 'teetering' configuration. Those rotors with hinge offset can either achieve this with actual mechanical flapping hinges or by the use of 'hingeless' hubs in which flexible structure bends as a hinge would. With mechanical hinges, the offset is generally less than about 5 per cent of the rotor radius, but with a hingeless rotor, the effective hinge offset may be up to 15 per cent. The offset affects the control power by generating a couple due to centrifugal forces at the hub that adds to the moment about the centre of gravity caused by the tilt of the thrust vector as the rotor flaps.

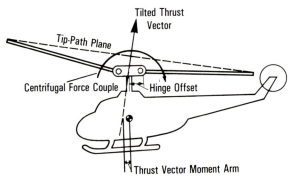

***Two Sources of Control Power***

The amount of the offset affects the control power as illustrated below.

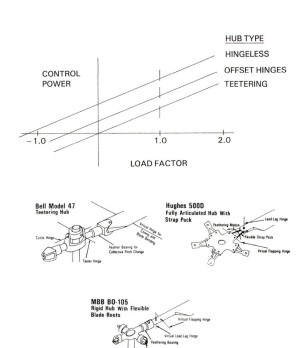

***Effect of Flapping Hinge Offset on Control Power***

The difference in control power between the various rotor configurations is generally not an important factor in normal flying. Most teetering rotors obtain adequate control power using only thrust vector tilt, although as a general rule, the designers have placed these rotors high to maximise this effect. The difference will be most important in non-standard flying when the rotor thrust is reduced. This, for instance, happens when flying close to rolling terrain as the pilot tries to descend rapidly into the next valley. During this low load factor manoeuvre, the low thrust reduces the control power available from blade flapping and in the extreme case can even result in zero or reversed control. A rotor with offset flapping hinges will retain the portion of its control power that is due to the centrifugal force couple even when the thrust is zero. The load factor at which the control power goes to zero is shown below as a function of the hinge offset ratio for a typical helicopter.

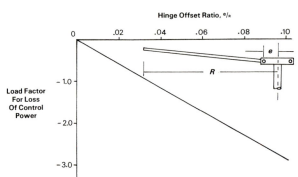

***Effect of Hinge Offset on Minimum Controllable Load Factor***

The amount of hinge offset also has an effect on turning capability. Except at very low speeds, most turns are done by banking, so the time required to turn is affected by the time to achieve the bank angle. The shortest time depends both on the maximum rate of roll and on the maximum roll acceleration. Each of these depend on different rotor parameters. The maximum rate of roll depends on the polar moment of inertia of the rotor and on the amount of lateral cyclic pitch built into the control system. It is essentially independent of rotor-hub type whether it be teetering, hinged, or hingeless. This is because when a steady rate of roll is established, the tip-path plane is close to being perpendicular to the rotor shaft. Any lateral flapping is only used to generate a roll moment to overcome the aerodynamic damping of the rest of the airframe which is generally very small. Any more flapping would generate a moment that would accelerate the fuselage, but no acceleration can exist if the roll rate has already reached a steady value. For this condition, if little or no flapping exists, it does not matter how the blades are attached to the hub.

The rate of roll may be independent of the hub type, but roll acceleration is not. The figure below shows the response to the same amount of cyclic pitch on three helicopters which are identical except for their hub configurations.

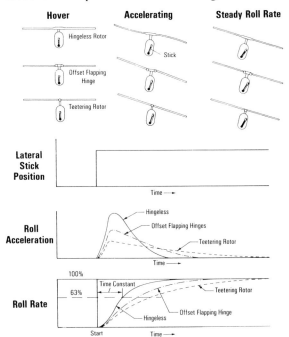

*Control Characteristics in Roll*

Even though all three eventually reach the same rate of roll, the one with the hingeless rotor reaches it first. The acceleration is quantified by reference to a 'time constant', which is the time required to achieve 63 per cent of the steady rate. The shorter the time constant, the 'crisper' will the manoeuvre feel to the pilot.

Although large amounts of hinge offset assure the crispness that pilots like, there are several negative considerations. A rotor is unstable with angle of attack. The instability is such that if the rotor encounters an up-gust, it will flap back applying a nose-up pitching moment to the helicopter that results in an even higher nose-up attitude. Designers use a horizontal stabiliser to counteract this rotor instability. The more the hinge offset, the higher will be the destabilising moment and the bigger the tail will have to be to balance it. More tail area means more drag and

more airframe weight at the aft end where it pulls the centre of gravity back, which in itself is bad for angle-of-attack stability.

Another consideration is that high hinge offset makes it easier to tip the helicopter over on the ground by inadvertently using too much lateral cyclic pitch even when the rotor is in flat pitch.

## The Lead-Lag Hinge

— Should be used to reduce in-plane blade stresses.

— Should not be used to simplify the hub and to avoid 'ground resonance'.

When Juan de la Cierva developed the flapping hinge for his autogiro, he solved the basic problem of a rotor flying through the air edgewise by allowing it to use a flapping motion to balance the asymmetric aerodynamics between the advancing and retreating blades. After flying the aircraft for some time, however, a new problem became apparent. The blades began to show structural distress from back-and-forth bending moments in the plane of the rotor. Simply because the lift was balanced around the rotor disc, did not mean that the drag was also balanced. Besides aerodynamic drag, there was a dynamic effect because the joint produced by the flapping hinges between the shaft and the rotor was not a constant-speed joint and as a result when the blades flapped, their inertia produced oscillating dynamic loads in the plane of the rotor.

When Cierva realised that the in-plane bending moment at the blade root was high enough to cause trouble, he naturally decided that if one hinge was good, two would be even better, so he installed a vertical pin in each blade that gave it the freedom to move back and forth; to lead and to lag. Even when cyclic pitch replaced flapping for trimming the rotor, the in-plane moments were high enough to justify retaining the lead-lag hinge and so many of today's helicopters – those with 'fully articulated' – rotors still carry them. Other rotors, especially of the two-bladed teetering type, do not use lead-lag hinges but rely instead on sufficient structural strength to withstand the in-plane moments. Hingeless rotors may or may not have some form of flexibility that takes the place of an actual mechanical lead-lag hinge. Whether actual or effective, if a lead-lag hinge is present, it must be provided with a damper to prevent a destructive form of dynamic instability known as 'ground resonance'.

*Sikorsky S-58 Hub is an example of a hub with loose attachments with mechanical hinges for flapping and lead-lag.*

## Rotor Hubs

— Should combine all the features that result in low weight, low drag, low cost, long life, easy maintenance, low part count, freedom from dynamic problems, adequate control power, and immunity to battle damage.

Since rotary-wing flight began, the design of rotor hubs has been one of the greatest chal-lenges. Many different configurations are used on current production and experimental heli-copters because the designers have not yet been able to design a hub that combines all of the desirable features. The first decision that must be made is how to handle the flapping, lead-lag, and feathering motions. The choices can vary from a very loose attachment with mechanical hinges for flapping and lead-lag and rotary feathering bearings to a rotor with no hinges or bearings at all.

An example of the first type may be found on Sikorsky helicopters designed between 1950 and 1970. These are 'fully articulated' hubs with obvious mechanical hinges.

A more recent design technology is used by Aerospatiale in which the necessary freedom to move has been achieved through flexibility in the arms of the hub and by attaching the blades to the hub with elastomeric blocks.

An even more recent design is that of Bell in which no sign of an actual hinge is to be seen. Here all the flapping, lead-lag, and feathering motions are accomplished in the bending and twisting of a 'flex-beam' that connects the blade to the hub.

Even with this demonstrated progress in rotor hub technology, no design team has yet devised a hub that meets all of the stated goals.

## Rotor Blade Airfoils

— Should be thin and flat for minimum com-pressibility effects on the advancing side.
— Should be thick and generously cambered for minimum stall effects on the retreating side.

*Aerospatiale Dauphin 2 hub on the SA 365M Panther.*

*The Bell 680 Hub.*

— Should have very low pitching moments in any flight condition.

Until someone develops a rotor on which the airfoil shape cyclically changes to simultaneously accommodate all of these requirements, designers are faced with choosing compromise airfoils.

After several decades of intense airfoil development for rotor blades, a 'generic' airfoil shape has emerged. Its characteristics are summarised below.

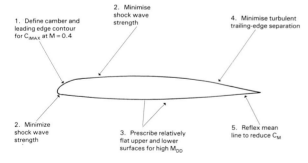

*The Characteristics of a Suitable Rotor Airfoil*

When blades were made from sheet metal, one airfoil section was generally used for the whole blade. With the advent of construction with composite materials, where the blade is made in a mould, it has become feasible to vary the shape along the blade to tailor it to the actual aerodynamic environment. Such a tailoring was done on the blades used on the record-breaking Westland Lynx.

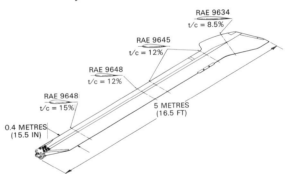

*Variation of Airfoils*

In this case, a thin airfoil was used at the very tip with which the special tip shape minimised both compressibility and stall problems. Inboard of the tip, where the Mach number is lower, a cambered airfoil was used to take advantage of its high stalling angle. Such an airfoil, though, has a high nose-down pitching moment so on the inboard portion of the blade was installed a similar airfoil but one with a reflexed trailing edge that produced a nose-up pitching moment to compensate.

# The Anti-Torque System

Not all helicopters need to balance the main rotor torque. A discussion of alternate 'torque-less' configurations will be found in the chapter on Other Configurations. Not all single main rotor configured helicopters use a conventional tail rotor. One design uses a small ducted fan in the fin and another a fan in the base of the tail boom with appropriate ducting to provide a force for anti-torque and for directional control. There is a very good reason for not using a tail rotor – it is a source of danger both to people and objects on the ground and to the helicopter itself. On the other hand, a tail rotor is the most effective way known to generate the required anti-torque force, and to provide good directional stability and control. For that reason, we shall first discuss the design decisions that must be made if a tail rotor is chosen; leaving discussions of the other systems for later.

## Tail Rotor Parameters

Just as for the main rotor, the tail rotor designer is faced with conflicting choices.

### Diameter

— Should be large to minimise the power required to generate the required anti-torque force and to provide good directional stability and control.
— Should be small to minimise the penalties of weight and to prevent an aft centre of gravity problem.

Although these conflicting desires would appear to leave every designer on his own, a study of existing helicopters indicates that there is a remarkably consistent relationship for the ratio of the diameter of the tail rotor to the main rotor as a function of main rotor disc loading as shown below.

There are probably three reasons for this

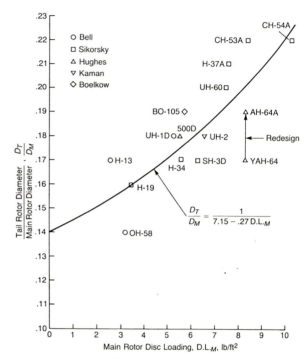

**Tail Rotor Sizing Trend**

consistency: Firstly, with a high disc loading, the main rotor requires so much power that saving power with a big tail rotor is attractive; secondly, with a low disc loading, the tail boom is very long and the difficulty of balancing the helicopter is made easier by using a small tail rotor; and finally, when looking at other helicopters, the observed trend becomes aesthetically pleasing.

### Vertical Location

— Should be low to minimise the weight and complexity of the tail rotor drive system.
— Should be high to provide good ground clearance, to increase stability in forward flight and, to minimise the lateral tilt of the helicopter in hover.

When the tail rotor is located right on the end of

**General Case**

Type of Main Rotor : With Some Hinge Offset

Height of Tail Rotor: Between CG and Main Rotor

Results _ Some Flapping Down to Left
            Some Fuselage Left Tilt

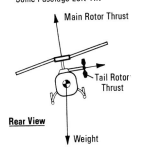

**Rear View**

| Special Cases | | | |
|---|---|---|---|
| Type of Main Rotor | Teetering | Any | Very High Offset |
| Height of Tail Rotor | As High as Main | As Low as CG | Any |
| Results | Fuselage Level | Fuselage Tilted, No Flapping | Fuselage Tilted, Very Little Flapping |

*Lateral Tilt in Hover*

the tail boom, only one gear box is required in its drive system. The low position has the disadvantage, however, that it is a danger to ground personnel and to the helicopter itself when doing nap-of-the-earth flight. When the rotor is mounted up on a vertical fin, an extra – or intermediate – gear box must be added with a cost and weight penalty.

The vertical location also has an influence on how much the helicopter must tilt laterally to trim in hover. Almost all single-rotor helicopters with counter-clockwise rotation of the main rotor hover with the left landing gear low. This is because the rightward thrust of the tail rotor must be balanced by leftward tilt of the main rotor. Besides gross weight and tail-rotor thrust, the degree of fuselage tilt depends on two physical parameters: the amount of hinge offset of the main rotor blades, and the vertical position of the tail rotor with respect to the main rotor and the aircraft's centre of gravity. The figure shows the rear view of four helicopters.

The first depicts a general case with some hinge offset and the tail rotor located between the main rotor and the centre of gravity. It has some fuselage tilt. Also shown are three special cases: one in which the parameters are arranged to produce no tilt by using a teetering rotor and a high tail rotor, and two others in which the fuselage is tilted as much as the tip path plane.

To minimise the fuselage tilt, the designer may choose to install the rotor mast with some compensating tilt. A value can be chosen that will be good for an average gross weight and not too bad for others.

Some helicopters appear to have weak directional stability around trim because the nose is continually 'hunting'. One reason for this is undoubtedly the turbulence in the air that surrounds the tail rotor and vertical stabiliser after it has been disturbed by the main rotor hub and the fuselage. Another reason may be found in the configuration of the flow field at the aft end of the helicopter as it is affected by the roll-up of the main rotor tip vortices as dramatically shown in the photograph of a crop dusting helicopter.

The flow near the bottom of the wake is directed outwards and the flow near the top, inwards. A tail rotor placed low will be in a region of diverging flow so that in a sideslip, it experiences less of a stabilising change of angle

*Flow Field at the Tail Rotor*

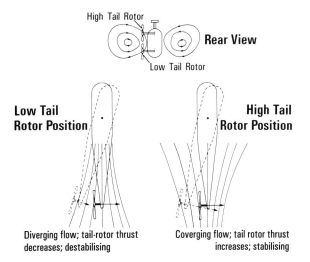

Low Tail Rotor Position — Diverging flow; tail-rotor thrust decreases; destabilising

High Tail Rotor Position — Coverging flow; tail rotor thrust increases; stabilising

of attack, and is therefore less effective, than had it been located high where the stabilising effect is actually increased.

## Tip Speed

— Should be low to minimise noise.
— Should be high to minimise weight.

Aerodynamic considerations are of less importance for the tail rotor than for the main rotor so choosing the tail rotor tip speed usually depends on the relative importance of noise and weight. Because the human ear is more sensitive to high frequencies than to low, the tail rotor can often be heard – at least at short ranges, above the sound of the main rotor even though it is putting far less energy into the air. Thus a low tip speed is desirable. On the other hand, compared to a low tip speed, a high one requires less blade area and lower torque through the tail rotor drive system, resulting in lower weight. Tail rotor tip speeds for current helicopter designs run from 527 ft/sec (160 m/s) for the optional quiet, four-bladed tail rotor available on the McDonnell Douglas ND500 series to 739 ft/sec on the Bell AH-1S Cobra.

## Blade Area and Airfoil Section

With the diameter and the tip speed chosen, the required blade area is not a subject of a tradeoff. It is fixed by the amount of thrust that is required to perform the anti-torque function and at the same time to provide a satisfactory margin of directional control under the worst conditions. This depends somewhat on the airfoil.

The basis for selection of the tail rotor airfoil is similar to that used on the main rotor and imposes the same dilemma. A thin, flat airfoil would be good for the advancing side to minimise compressibility problems at high speeds, but a thick, cambered airfoil would be desirable on the retreating side to minimise problems caused by stall. Since tail rotor blades are usually stubbier and therefore torsionally stiffer than main rotor blades, the danger of subjecting them to large pitching moments is less and for that reason, designers tend to choose on the side of the thick airfoils to take advantage of their higher maximum lift capabilities.

Choosing the total blade area depends on how the engine power, and thus the required anti-torque force, changes with altitude. The design condition will be a full power vertical climb either at sea level where the engine power is high or at high altitude where the air density is low. The tail rotor should generate enough thrust, without stalling, to provide the necessary anti-torque force with a 10 per cent margin for manoeuvring.

## Number of Blades

— Should be low to minimise cost.
— Should be high to minimise tip losses.

Dividing the required blade area into actual blades is the next decision. The fewer the blades, the cheaper the rotor will be to build and to maintain but if this results in very stubby blades, the high tip losses may penalise the performance. Most designers will select the number of blades that result in a blade aspect ratio (radius/chord) of between five and nine.

## Twist

— Should be high for good hover performance.
— Should be low for ease of construction and for minimum thrust variations in the vortex ring state.

High twist is beneficial for improving the hovering performance and in delaying retreating blade stall at high speed on the tail rotor just as it is on the main rotor. It may, however, complicate the construction of short, metal blades and it seems to make it more difficult to hold a constant heading in left sideward flight (for helicopters on which the main rotor is turning counter-clockwise) when the tail rotor is in the vortex ring state.

## Maximum Pitch

— Should be just enough to provide the required manoeuvreability in all flight conditions; but no higher.

The maximum pitch requirement is that which allows the helicopter to turn against main rotor torque from its most critical steady flight condition. For most helicopters this will be while doing right sideward flight at the highest gross weight and operational altitude where the tail rotor pitch must be high enough to generate the required thrust while at the same time compensating for the high inflow due to the sideward speed. Designing in too much pitch control may lead to a problem when stopping a fast hover turn in the direction in which the main rotor torque assists. For a turn in this direction, the tail rotor blade pitch is very low. If the turn is stopped abruptly with maximum available opposite pitch, the angle of attack will momentarily be equal to the pitch since the induced velocity requires a finite time to develop. If the angle of attack is above the stall angle of the airfoil, the tail rotor will momentarily demand very high power, perhaps more than the drive system was designed to deliver.

## Direction of Rotation

Before 1960, designers chose whatever direction of rotation for the tail rotor they wanted. Since then, the results of a number of projects have shown that there is a right way and a wrong way to turn the tail rotor. The right way is with the tail rotor blade closest to the main rotor going up. For reasons that are not well understood, this direction minimises the thrust fluctuations of the tail rotor in sideward flight when it is operating in the vortex ring state. It also minimises noise in forward flight due to the tail rotor cutting through the wake of the main rotor.

## Pushers and Pullers

Most modern helicopters use a vertical fin to augment the directional stability of the tail rotor. For greater effectiveness, these two components should be located at the end of the tail boom, but if they are too close together, their mutual interference hurts both. If too far apart, however, the assembly will be heavy.

Interference in hover depends upon which side of the fin the tail rotor is mounted, ie does it blow air on the fin or does it suck air past it? Since the induced velocity 'below' the tail rotor is higher than above, the drag of the fin is higher if the tail rotor is blowing on it. This reduces the effective net thrust of the tail rotor for anti-torque purposes. The relative power penalty is shown below for both 'tractor' and 'pusher' arrangements.

For the counter-clockwise sense of main rotor rotation, the pusher tail rotor is mounted on the left side of the fin. Almost all tail rotors are of the pusher type. The outstanding exceptions are the Sikorsky S-70A/UH-60A and the later Bell UH-1s and AH-1s. The S-70A designers chose to cant the tail rotor so that part of its thrust helps lift the rear end of the aircraft. To provide

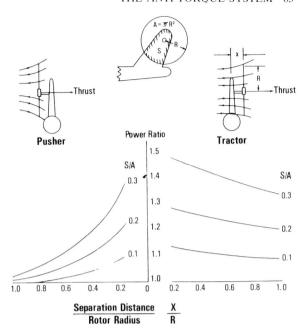

*Tail Rotor Power Penalty Due to Blockage*

clearance with the fin without using a long driveshaft, the tractor configuration was chosen. In Bell's case, the configuration comes about from changing the direction of rotation from the wrong way to the right way during the production run. The rotation was reversed simply by changing the mounting of the tail rotor from the left side to the right side of the fin. The Soviets appear to have discovered the problem as is evidenced by the fact that Mil used the Bell solution on both the Mi8/14/17 series and on the Mi-24 'Hind' where in each case, the tail rotor was switched from the right side to the left. (The main rotor, of course, turns in the 'Russian' direction.)

## Blade Retention

How to attach the blades and hub to the tail rotor shaft is a decision that has to be made early in the design process. In forward flight, the tail rotor wants to flap, something that is permitted in all designs since it has been found to be impractical to prevent it. The simplest way to permit flapping is to use a teetering hinge on two-bladed rotors or individual flapping hinges on multi-bladed rotors. The McDonnell Douglas AH-64A appears to have a four-bladed tail rotor, but it is actually two two-bladed teetering rotors mounted about six inches apart.

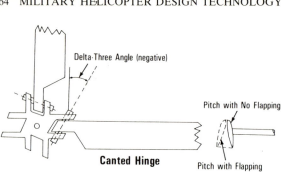

**Canted Hinge**

Delta-Three Angle (negative)

Pitch with No Flapping

Pitch with Flapping

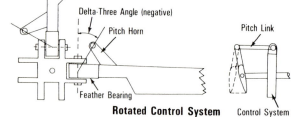

**Rotated Control System**

Delta-Three Angle (negative)

Pitch Horn

Pitch Link

Feather Bearing

Control System

*Two Methods of Obtaining Pitch/Flap Coupling*

## Cant

Sikorsky designers have used tail rotors canted 20 degrees down to the left on both the S-70 and the CH-53E. This is to take advantage of the upward component of tail rotor thrust to help hold the helicopter up in hover and to help trim an aft centre of gravity position. The disadvantage is that pedal in-puts produce pitching moments that must be compensated for by elaborate mechanical decouplings in the control system.

# Other Anti-Torque Configurations

Fenestron: A tail rotor is dangerous to ground personnel and to the helicopter itself when operating close to obstructions. It also has a significant radar signature. If the tail rotor could be reduced in size and surrounded with structure, these problems could be minimised. Several

*Aerospatiale's Fenestron on a Gazelle.*

Most tail rotors are designed with some amount of mechanical coupling that changes the pitch of the blade as it flaps. This is done either by canting the flapping hinge or by locating the joint between the pitch horn and the pitch link off the hinge line. Both possibilities are shown below.

This coupling is referred to as 'delta-three', a term invented by the autogiro designers who identified and named several possible types of kinetic rotor couplings. If the pitch increases as the blade flaps up, it is positive delta-three. Both positive and negative values have been used on tail rotors with the negative being most common. The main reason for using either positive or negative delta-three coupling is that it simplifies the layout of the control system, reducing possible mechanical interferences and making for shorter and lighter components. Another reason is that by changing the blade's natural frequency away from resonance, it reduces transient blade loads.

Several recent tail rotor designs have no mechanical hinges but use flex-beams made of composite materials to provide the flexibility needed to minimise the moments and loads. For these, the correct delta-three coupling becomes important in maintaining stability of some of the dynamic modes.

attempts have been made to do this but the only one to get into production at this writing is the 'fenestron' developed by Aerospatiale for use on their Gazelle and Dauphin series. (A fenestron is a small round window in French houses.)

By shaping the hole like a duct, the designers can get a performance benefit corresponding to a somewhat larger diameter since the lips of the duct produce a low static pressure that adds to the force generated by the fan. Whether the force is produced by the fan or by the lips of the duct, the total force and power required to develop it are related to the energy in the fully developed wake. A conventional rotor has a wake that requires some distance to contract to its final diameter which is 70 per cent of the size of the rotor. By putting a duct around the rotor, the wake is effectively matured in the duct and undergoes no further contraction downstream. Thus the fenestron can produce the same total thrust for the same power as a tail rotor which is 30 per cent larger. The benefit is even higher if the duct has a slight divergence to expand the wake and if the comparable tail rotor suffers a

*The US Coast Guard's HH-65A also uses the fenestron anti-torque device.*

blockage penalty by being too close to its supporting fin.

Aerospatiale engineers claim that with these considerations, the fenestron fan diameter can be as small as 50 per cent of the tail rotor it is replacing; but up to now they have been using even smaller diameter fans, thus decreasing the power available for the main rotor. Since it is difficult to enclose a fan big enough to match the tail rotor, the tradeoff decision is a difficult one; safety versus performance. It may be significant that Aerospatiale chose to use a tail rotor rather than a fenestron on the AS350 Ecureuil, the model following the Dauphin.

As with a tail rotor, the larger the diameter of the fenestron, the less power required to generate the needed thrust. A practical illustration of this is found in the development of the Aerospatiale HH-65A Dolphin for the US Coast Guard. The original contract was for an off-the-shelf version of the Dauphin 2, but it was found to be deficient in hover performance. Aerospatiale solved the problem by increasing the diameter of the fan from 35 to 43 inches (89 cm to 109 cm) which resulted in a hover improvement corresponding to about 260 lbs (118 kg) of additional allowable payload. The HH-65A has the company designation of SA 366G1.

According to theory, the depth of the duct should be at least 20 per cent of the fan diameter to be fully effective in hover. This means that it is difficult to streamline the device for low drag in forward flight. It also means that the airpath into and out of the fan is tortuous so its efficiency is penalised. For this reason, the fenestron is always integrated with a generously sized cambered vertical fin that can take over the job of torque compensation in forward flight. This has the advantage of decreasing the loads on the blades and drive system, thus prolonging the lives of these components.

Even with the fenestron, the direction of rotation has been found important. Directional control problems on the Gazelle, which has the fan blade closest to the main rotor going down, were much reduced on the Dauphin, for which the rotation was reversed.

## Fan-in-Boom

Another possibility for eliminating the danger of a tail rotor and reducing the radar signature of the anti-torque device is a concept using a pressurised tail boom. As developed by McDonnell Douglas Helicopters, and called 'NOTAR' for *NO TAil Rotor*, it consists of a controllable-pitch fan installed just aft of the transmission blowing air down the hollow tail boom to a nozzle with a set of 90° turning vanes. The reaction of the flow against the vanes produces an anti-torque force.

*A modified 0H-6 with NOTAR.*

Both the pitch of the fan and the size of the nozzle opening are controlled by the pilot's pedal movements. In hover, another contribution to the anti-torque force is provided by the circulation-control tail boom. This concept makes use of the deflection of the main rotor wake as it passes the boom through the influence of sheets of air blowing from two slots on the lower right hand side.

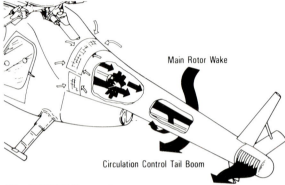

*The NOTAR Concept*

The jets of air come out nearly tangential to the boom's surface and entrain the boundary layer on the right side – delaying its separation and bending the whole wake flow to the left. This distortion of the wake produces suction on the right side of the boom which according to theory should provide nearly two-thirds of the required anti-torque force in hover. In forward flight, where the wake does not impinge on the boom, the necessary forces come from the deflected jet and the cambered vertical stabiliser.

# Empennages and Wings

The designers of the first helicopters were delighted just to see them get off of the ground. If they even thought about stability and control, the emphasis was on the latter, as was the case with the Wright Brothers when they developed their unstable but very controllable 'Flier'. Consequently, if the early helicopters had any tail surfaces at all, they were of minimum size, but as the helicopter grew so did both the horizontal and vertical stabilising surfaces. The need for such surfaces is the same as with aeroplanes: a streamline fuselage shape is unstable in both pitch and yaw and the addition of a wing or a rotor makes it even more so.

## Horizontal Stabiliser

### Location

The first task is to decide where this surface should be placed. One of the prime considerations is the effect the location will have on the longitudinal trim when going from hover to forward flight. If the pilot must rapidly displace his longitudinal cyclic control forward to keep the aircraft from pitching nose-up, it is probably caused by the sudden impingement of the main rotor wake on the horizontal stabiliser which in hover is behind the wake but is inside it at low forward speeds. This was not a problem when horizontal surfaces were small and main rotor disc loadings were low, but in recent years, designers have used larger tails and more highly loaded rotors so that the potential for serious aerodynamic interaction problems has increased. From an examination of the side view drawing of a given helicopter, it is not too difficult to anticipate a potential problem in this regard. Designers have taken three different approaches to the solution of this problem.

Designers at Bell have generally placed horizontal stabilisers forward on the tail boom so that they are in the wake in hover and never have an awkward transition going from outside

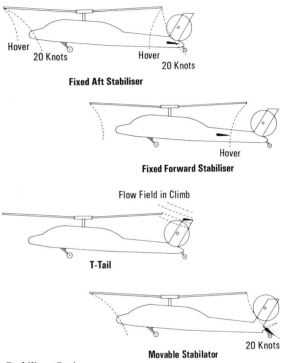

*Stabiliser Options*

the wake to inside it. This option hampers hover performance because of the download and because more tail area is required for stability than if it were mounted further back.

Another approach is the T-tail configuration used by Sikorsky on its large helicopters and by McDonnell Douglas on its small ones. This puts the surface high enough that it is above the rotor wake except at very high speeds. It has been found, however, that unless the tail is placed very high, the download may still be high at low speed, especially in climbs. This installation may also put the surface inside the main rotor wake at high speed where the induced turbulence may cause dynamic problems. Finally, this arrangement is heavy because of its structural inefficiency.

Yet another modern solution is to mount a variable-incidence 'stabilator' at the end of the tail boom. (The term comes from the description of the all-flying tails used on many modern aeroplanes where the movable surface takes the place of both the stabiliser and the elevator). This surface can then be aligned with the flow in the wake at low speeds to minimise the airloads. This solves the trim problem but results in additional weight, cost, complexity, and the danger that the stabilator control system might do the wrong thing at the wrong time such as going to the nose-up hover position while flying at high speed. The low location may also put the surface directly behind rockets or missiles mounted on the fuselage or on a wing. These weapons eject pieces of wire and plastic plugs to the rear with enough velocity to dent a conventional aluminum structure. It may, therefore, be found necessary to protect the leading edge of the stabilator with a sheet of rubber as is done on the AH-64A.

It can be seen from this discussion, that none of the options produce a truly satisfactory installation, but perhaps that is just for helicopters as we know them today. On the horizon are advanced control systems with which the pilot uses his cockpit control to accelerate and then hold a desired velocity. An effective system of this type should automatically, and independently of the pilot, put in the correct cyclic pitch required to keep the helicopter in trim while flying through the transition region even with variable loads on a fixed horizontal stabiliser.

Aerodynamic Considerations: Any component mounted at the end of the tail boom operates in a poor environment because of what the air has experienced before it reached there. These experiences include: being pushed aside by the fuselage, engine nacelles, shaft, and rotor hub; being slowed down by skin friction; losing momentum and gaining turbulence through flow separation; picking up exhaust gases; and being vigorously stirred by the rotating blades, hub, and control rods. It is no wonder, therefore, that by the time the air gets to the aft end of the fuselage, it is not only tired but is also confused about which way it should be going. Both the tiredness and the confusion can be measured during a flow survey during a wind tunnel test. The figure below shows the result of one such survey for a model with a powered main rotor in terms of the loss of dynamic pressure at the empennage position.

The next figure shows the rear view of the measured flow vectors.

The flow environment described by these two figures obviously affects the handling qualities of

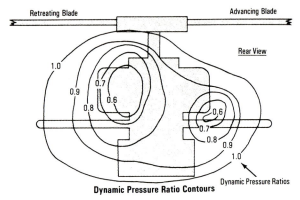

**Loss of Dynamic Pressure at the Empennage**

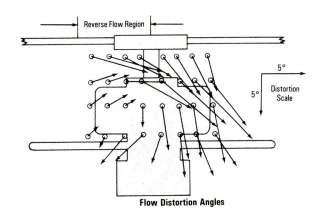

*Flow Direction*

the helicopter. The regions of low dynamic pressure decrease the effectiveness of stabilising surfaces located in them both because of the low dynamic pressure and because they represent regions in which the flow tends to align itself with the fuselage and so the surfaces are not subjected to full angle of attack changes as the aircraft pitches and yaws.

Both the effects of downwash and swirl are reflected in the second figure that shows that most of the vectors are pointed down and to the right. Two more features of the wake are evident: the much stronger downwash behind the advancing side than behind the reverse flow region on the retreating side, and the beginning of the roll-up of the rotor tip vortices as evidenced by the curvature of the vectors on the right-hand side. Not only are the tip vortices important in defining the flow at the tail, but the less-well-understood root vortices are undoubtedly doing their share to mix it up.

The flow measurements summarised in the figures represent only average conditions in a flow field that also has a large amount of unsteadiness which on several helicopters has led to serious 'tail shake' problems. Some of the unsteadiness is at the frequency of blade passage as each blade generates its own contribution to the flow field. If the structural natural frequencies of the tail boom and/or of the stabilising surfaces are near the blade passage frequency or multiples of it, the tail shake problem may be serious enough to require structural modifications.

Some of the aerodynamic excitation may be of a more random nature as generated by unsteady flow separation around the main rotor mast fairing. As a general rule, this problem can not be anticipated during the design phase, it only becomes evident during flight test. As an engineering fix, the local flow can be made steadier by installing a special fairing between the upper fuselage and the bottom of the rotor hub that will act as a small wing to generate tip vortices that will organise the air flow on the neighbouring structure and in the air as it approaches the tail surfaces. Even further organisation can be done by also installing a fairing at the top of the rotor hub as shown in the Aerospatiale sketch below.

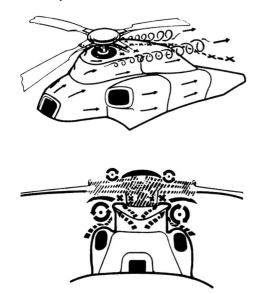

**Vortex Patterns from Pylon and Hub Fairings**

The improvement in the flow field does not come free, however. The energy in the vortices must come from some place and shows up in the detailed bookkeeping as airframe induced drag. For this reason, these two devices should be installed only after initial flight testing shows that a significant tail shake problem exists.

Another problem that is difficult to anticipate during the design because of the chaotic flow near the empennage is the longitudinal trim change when going from one power condition to another such as from a full-power climb to auto-rotation at the same airspeed. A helicopter, unlike an aeroplane, climbs and descends at a nearly level-fuselage attitude as shown below.

*Trim Conditions in Climb and Descent*

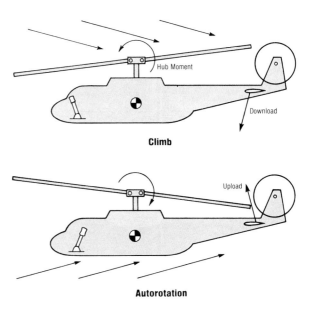

This characteristic puts the horizontal stabiliser through a wide angle of attack range from large negative in climb to high positive in descent. Consequently, the stabiliser develops a download in climb, producing a nose-up pitching moment about the helicopter's centre of gravity. Conversely, in descent, the load is up and the pitching moment nose-down. The pilot must use rotor flapping to balance these moments; so he holds the cyclic stick forward in climbs and aft in descents. If the stick travel required to go from trim in a full-power climb to autorotation at the same airspeed is more than about three inches, the characteristic is judged to be unsatisfactory.

One approach used to minimise the adverse trim shift is to change the high angle of attack characteristics of the stabiliser with aerodynamic modifications. This can be seen on many helicopters in the form of an inverted-cambered airfoil that stalls at relatively low positive angles of attack. This limits the amount of upload that

*The Bell UH-1 Stabiliser.*

*The Aerospatiale Super Puma Stabiliser.*

the surface can generate in auto-rotation. If this is not sufficient, a spoiler on the upper surface can be added as can be seen on the Bell UH-1 series.

Once a stabiliser stalls, either in descent or in climb, it loses its effectiveness as a stabilising surface, since changes in angle of attack are not accompanied by corresponding changes in lift. This has resulted in degraded flying qualities for

some helicopters. The most troublesome condition has been in climb where the stabiliser is working at large negative angles of attack. To prevent stalling in this condition, several modern helicopters use fixed leading-edge slats to control the flow around the nose, thus permitting larger negative angles before stall. This configuration can now be seen on the Bell 222 and on the Aerospatiale Super Puma.

The other approach which solves the trim change problem while maintaining the surface as an effective stabiliser is to use a movable stabilator with its incidence controlled not only

*Stabilator Incidence Schedule for McDonnell Douglas Apache*

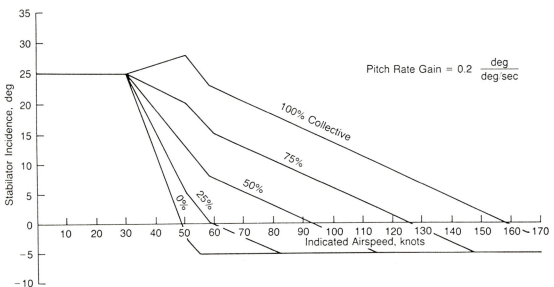

by forward speed but also by main rotor collective pitch position.

With this type of system, the stabilator goes nose-up in a climb and nose-down in a descent thus at least approximately compensating for the change in the flow field.

For the initial General Arrangement drawing, the designer can take as a guide for sizing the horizontal stabiliser what it is that looks about right based on previous helicopters. As the design matures, the stability and control engineer will recommend resizing by considering the predicted stability characteristics of the fuselage and rotor as he learns about them through analysis and wind tunnel tests.

# Vertical Stabiliser

In many cases, the tail rotor alone is effective enough to give a helicopter directional stability without the need for a vertical stabiliser; but most modern designs have one nonetheless. Depending on the helicopter, the vertical stabiliser may: streamline the tail rotor support, supplement the directional stability produced by the tail rotor, unload the tail rotor in forward flight by providing some anti-torque force, support a T-tail, or stabilise a fuselage in case the tail rotor is shot off completely.

A vertical stabiliser above the tail boom is in dirty air in level flight, but in descent the situation is even worse. For several helicopter designs, initial flight testing of the prototype has shown poor directional stability in descents. One fix has been to add a ventral fin under the tail boom where in descent, the environment is improving when that of the upper fin is deteriorating. Those helicopters with the tail rotor located directly on the end of the tail boom generally start out with some sort of ventral fin which may be nothing more than a streamline fairing over the structure that protects the tail rotor from striking the ground during a landing flare.

Because of the low dynamic pressure behind the fuselage and hub and the tendency for the flow to stay parallel to the tail boom, some helicopter designers have chosen to place the vertical surfaces on the ends of the horizontal stabiliser. This is also a convenient place to add more area in case flight test shows that it is

*Evolution of an Endplate Configuration: the MBB 104 (above) and BK 117 (below).*

desirable since it can be done with a minimum of structural changes. An example of this can be seen in the comparison of the empennages of the BO 105 and the BK 117.

*Two truncated vertical stabilisers: UH-60A Black Hawk (top) and AH-64A Apache (bottom)*

The original intent, in the interest of commonality, was that the tail boom, tail rotor, and empennage would be the same on both aircraft. Flight tests of the heavier and larger-bodied BK-117, however, showed that in some flight conditions, the directional stability needed improving and so the much larger endplates were installed.

Besides getting the vertical surfaces into cleaner air, endplates have two other aerodynamic advantages: they increase the effectiveness of the horizontal stabiliser by increasing its effective aspect ratio and they minimise the interference in hover between the tail rotor and the vertical surfaces. This configuration, however, is heavier than one with all of the area concentrated in a centrally located fin and may introduce dynamic problems by lowering the structural natural frequency of the assembly into the range of excitation frequencies of the main or tail rotor.

As long as the vertical surface is there, it might as well be used to its fullest. For this reason, many modern helicopters have cambered or cocked vertical surfaces that produce an anti-torque force in forward flight to help unload the tail rotor. The primary purpose is to reduce its flapping and thereby to minimise its oscillatory loads. The total anti-torque power required will probably be about the same, since the induced drag of the vertical surface absorbs the power that would otherwise be used to produce high tail rotor thrust.

Some recent military specifications have asked the designers to configure the aircraft so it could be flown home in case the tail rotor were completely shot off. By sideslipping, a big enough vertical stabiliser can produce sufficient anti-torque force to do this. Unfortunately, several development programmes have shown that such a big vertical stabiliser interferes with the performance of the tail rotor in sideward flight. As a consequence, the requirement has not been satisfied on such helicopters as the Sikorsky UH-60A or the McDonnell Douglas AH-64A where the evidence that portions of the vertical fins were deleted during development may still be seen in the production aircraft.

# The Wing

The question of including a wing in the configuration is often raised during the preliminary design phase. A wing is a convenient place to hang external stores or to carry fuel, but from an aerodynamic standpoint, it is always detrimental in hover because of its weight and download and usually also in forward flight. This is because the unloaded rotor will have to be tilted further forward to overcome the helicopter and wing drag resulting in higher angles of attack on the retreating tip leading to premature blade stall. Most designers agree that wings belong on a helicopter only if needed to provide a place to carry external stores or if they are used in conjunction with some sort of auxiliary propulsion to achieve higher speeds than are possible with a conventional helicopter.

If a wing is to be used, its incidence should be chosen so that at high speed it is operating at its best angle of attack. By analogy with biplanes, for minimum induced drag, the wing and rotor should be sharing lift such that the ratio of rotor lift to wing lift is equal to the square of rotor diameter divided by the square of the wing span.

The wing should be located with its aerodynamic centre behind the most aft centre of gravity position of the helicopter so that it acts as a stabiliser rather than a destabiliser.

A large wing may cause a problem in autorotation. If the wing supports a large portion of the gross weight, the rotor will be starved for thrust and will not be able to maintain autorotation. If this situation is possible, some means of reducing wing lift will have to be used, such as reverse flaps, spoilers, or incidence changes.

# The Geometric and Structural Layout

## The General Arrangement Drawing

### The Reference System

Knowing the diameter of the main and tail rotors, the designer begins his first (but not his last) version of the General Arrangement Drawing. Working drawings for ships were once laid out full-sized in lofts above the shops, and the word 'lofting' is still used when making drawings of aircraft, even when done on computers. One important reference for ship designers is the 'waterline' which means just what it says. Aircraft designers also use a horizontal reference which they call a waterline, but instead of making it come in the middle of the fuselage as it does in the middle of a hull, it comes well below so that each point on the aircraft will have a positive location. For the same reason, the zero fuselage station is placed well forward of the nose. For convenience most designers will chose the reference system so that the centre of the main rotor hub is at some easy-to-remember position; for example, the hub of the AH-64 was originally located at fuselage station 200 and waterline 200 (in inches). The other dimension is the 'buttline' that will appear in the front and top views as the lateral position of a component. In this case, the zero reference will be at the fuselage plane of symmetry and buttlines are designated either right or left, with the orientation established by looking forward.

Orienting the side view of the helicopter fuselage with the zero waterline is quite arbitrary. If the fuselage is a long cylinder as on a tandem rotor helicopter, it is obvious that its axis should be parallel to the master waterline, but on other helicopter shapes the designer has some freedom. In the past, he often chose some flat surface, such as a cabin floor, as being parallel to

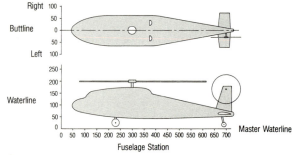

*Typical Lofting Scheme*

the waterline no matter what the fuselage shape turned out to be and then drew in the rotor mast tilted 3 to 5 degrees forward in recognition of the best fuselage angle of attack for low drag at high speed.

A better suggestion is to draw the mast vertical and then to tilt the fuselage shape slightly nose-up to achieve the same forward flight fuselage angle of attack. This is because the rotor shaft is one of the most important reference lines for analysis of aerodynamics, centre of gravity position, and moments of inertia. The use of this convention will also keep the centre of the rotor hub on that easy-to-remember fuselage station in case the rotor has to be raised during some subsequent redesign.

## Tail Rotor Location

The tail rotor can either be located right on the end of the tail boom or placed higher on a vertical fin. The considerations for each of these locations was discussed earlier.

## Main Rotor-Fuselage Proximity

A requirement for both the UTTAS and AAH helicopters procured by the US Army was that they could be transported in a C-130 or C-141 transport aircraft to the scene of the action and then prepared for flight in not more than 30 minutes. Both of these aircraft have 8 ft (2.44 m) high cargo compartments so the helicopter designers had good motivation to hold the height of their designs in a transportable configuration to this dimension.

Sikorsky and Boeing were the competitors for UTTAS and Hughes and Bell for the AAH. All used a 'kneeling' landing gear to minimise the height and all but Bell located their rotors down close to the top of the fuselage in order to meet the requirement. (Bell designed an ingenious scheme for telescoping the mast into the transmission for the AH-63). The three companies who chose to place their rotors in close proximity

to the fuselage all found difficulties arising from this choice. Both of the UTTAS prototypes were plagued by high vibration which at least partially came from blade loads induced by the up-flow of the air over the forward part of the fuselage. Both raised the rotor by lengthening the rotor mast thus minimising the effects of the up-flow but also making it necessary to remove the rotor and transmission in order to transport the helicopter in an eight-foot high cargo compartment.

The Hughes YAH-64 did not suffer from high vibration from the upflow over the nose, probably because the fuselage was much narrower than those of the UTTAS designs. It was found, however that when this aircraft started a push-over manoeuvre, the blades came down over the nose far enough to graze the top of the canopy. To cure this unacceptable situation, the mast was lengthened first ten inches in the prototypes and, then after further testing, another 6 in (152 mm)

*Changes to the UTTAS designs included mast-raisings on the Boeing YUH-61A, the unsuccessful contender.*

*After mast-raising: the UN-60A Black Hawk in US Army service.*

*Before mast-raising: the YUH-60A prototype which won UTTAS competition.*

*Changes to the AH-64 concept: before the*
*mast-raising (left) on the YAH-64 and after,*
*(right), on the AH-64A Apache.*

for production. This change forced a disassembly for transport on a C-130 Hercules or a C-141 Starlifter (but not a C-5 Galaxy).

A benefit of raising the rotors on all of these helicopters was the reduction in cockpit noise due to 'canopy drumming' as the blades passed over.

As a final note of caution about blade-airframe clearance, it should be noted that care must be used in designing upward-opening canopy doors or inspection panels that could be struck by blades during maintenance or if inadvertently opened during flight.

## Blade Clearance

When hinged, flexible blades are free to bend and to flap. Centrifugal forces tend to keep them straight and in a position nearly perpendicular to the shaft, but there are aerodynamic and dynamic forces that tend to move them out of this position. For clearance between the blades and the rest of the airframe, one of the most critical situations is when the helicopter is in contact

with the ground either firmly or in the last stages of a landing. In flight, the moments on the airframe that accompany blade flapping will tend to move the helicopter out of the way of the rotor (not always fast enough), but on the ground it will have no way to escape. At low rotor speeds, it is more likely to be a gust or the wake from a nearby helicopter that induces high flapping, but when the rotor is up to full operating speed, it is inadvertant cyclic pitch control inputs that may cause the blades to strike the fuselage. The amount of forward cyclic pitch that is designed into the control system depends primarily on the high speed goal of the helicopter. It must be enough to trim the rotor aerodynamically at the maximum speed with some margin for manoeuvreing. The rearward cyclic pitch must be enough to trim in rearward flight and/or to make a nose-up flare for a quick stop or a landing from autorotation. A survey of existing helicopters indicate that forward cyclic pitch of 20° and aft of 15° covers the range currently used. On the ground, the rotor flapping will be equal to these angles if the pilot

*The AH-64 Blade Clearance Problem*

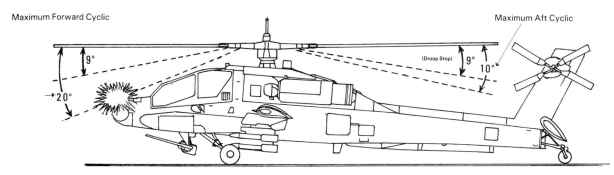

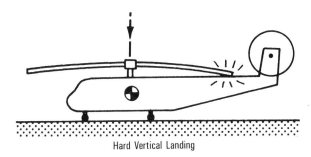

Hard Vertical Landing

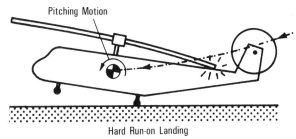

Hard Run-on Landing

***Possible Conditions During a Landing Flare***

inadvertently moves his cyclic stick to the stops. In most rotors, the flapping motion at the flapping hinges is restricted to some lower value than the maximum cyclic pitch by a 'droop stop'. This being so close to the hinges, however, is relatively ineffective against the large aerodynamic forces acting on the outboard portion and so the blade will bend around the droop stop almost as if it were not there. Thus to be absolutely safe, the clearance angles for fore and aft blade flapping should be at least as large as the fore and aft cyclic pitch provided. In the

***The S-55 Tail Boom Change (before canting tail boom down 3 degrees).***

past, this rule-of-thumb has not generally been observed on the assumption that no pilot would inadvertently use full cyclic pitch on the ground. However, it has happened and several cases of both fore and aft blade strikes have been attributed to this cause.

The AH-64 has 20 degrees of forward cyclic pitch. Although seldom used in flight, there have been at least two incidents on the ground where enough forward cyclic was inadvertently imposed to make the blade flap down over the nose far enough to contact the sight for the Pilot's Night Vision Device.

A tail boom strike is a too usual type of accident. A common situation has been as the helicopter was making a hard landing following autorotation. There are two contributing factors for these accidents: the blades which keep on coming down even after the fuselage has stopped, and the sudden nose-down motion following the contact of aft-mounted wheels or the back of skids which makes the pilot naturally want to pull the stick back to counteract it.

An example of a redesign forced by tail boom strikes was the Sikorsky S-55 (H-19) which originally had the tail boom coming straight out of the main fuselage. After a series of accidents in operation, it was redesigned with the tail boom angled down three degrees.

Tail boom strikes have also happened in flight. The most common scenario is that during the entry to autorotation as the collective pitch is lowered, the rotor flaps forward since the advancing blade sees a greater reduction in lift than does the retreating blade. The pilot over-reacts to the sudden nose-down pitching moment by suddenly pulling the cyclic stick back. With this action, the rotor flaps back, but the tail boom is still rising because of the initial aircraft nose-down motion. With insufficient clearance, a blade strike is the result.

Lateral flapping to the limits of lateral cyclic pitch (usually not more than ten degrees) generally will not cause a blade strike unless the helicopter is equipped with extremely long wings, but for rotors with large hinge offsets, too much lateral flapping may cause the helicopter to roll over on the ground. Some helicopters have been equipped with stick locks that are either manually put in place or automatically activated through mechanisms sensing landing gear compression to guard against these types of accidents.

When the rotor is up to full speed, gusts are generally less critical than cyclic pitch, but at low rotor speeds during a start-up or a shut-down, gusts are of concern since the blade is free to flap and bend without the stiffening effects of strong centrifugal forces. For very low rotor speeds, the aerodynamic forces are much less than at full rotor speed and the droop stops are of some value. Many rotors have spring-loaded, centrifugally-operated droop stops that prevent the blades from going below the height of the rotor hub until the rotor speed is near its operating value. Despite this there have been incidents of tail boom strikes during start-ups and shut-downs in a high wind or when another helicopter was landing or even taxiing nearby. The US Army requires that the rotor can be safely started and stopped in 45 kts (83 km/h) wind, while the US Navy requires a 60 kts (111 km/h) capability.

Even while parked, rotor blades may want to fly. At least one incident occured when one helicopter landed beside another: the recirculating rotor wake lifted a blade on the parked helicopter which then suddenly dropped against its droop stop leaving a permanent bend about two thirds the way out. To guard against this possibility, the designer should provide some means of tying the blades down or quickly folding and stowing them after landing.

## Tail Rotor Clearance

The tail rotor does not have a cyclic pitch system so it flaps or teeters in response to collective pitch, sideslip, and yaw rate. Unlike the main rotor in flight, the tail rotor cannot move the tail boom out of the way as it flaps and so there have been incidents in which a tail rotor mounted on a too-short shaft flapped enough to strike fixed structure during rapid pedal inputs at high speeds. To guard against this possibility on a new helicopter, the designer should enlist the help of the aerodynamicist who can estimate the maximum tail rotor flapping under the worst conditions.

## Folding It Up

Helicopters designed for ship-board operation and some others are required to be quickly stowed in the smallest possible space. Blade folding, either manually or automatically, is the first requirement, but it may also be necessary to fold the tail boom. Making all the parts nest gracefully together may be a challenging problem in descriptive geometry.

## Ground Clearance

Two conditions are important when discussing ground clearance: the nose-up attitude in a landing flare, and operation from sloping surfaces. During a landing flare, the pilot should have confidence that he is either not going to strike the aft end – including the tail rotor – on the ground or if he does, that the structure has been designed to take the resulting loads. In the latter case, the designer has provided a sturdy tail wheel and a strong tail boom such as on the Black Hawk and Apache. Without this provision, the designer must allow for an adequate flare angle between the main wheels or the aft end of the skids and the end of the tail boom. The consensus is that this should be no less than 10°.

During operation from sloping surfaces, the pilot must have the assurance that only those parts of the aircraft that he wants to touch the ground are doing so. This applies particularly to guns and missiles that might be hung under a wing. Since a single-rotor helicopter hovers with the left side low (with counter-clockwise main rotor rotation), landing on a side-slope rising to the left is a condition that must be investigated for adequate clearance.

## Ground Attitude

Because the initial takeoff and the final landing are almost always pure vertical manoeuvres, the helicopter should rest on the ground with its main rotor shaft vertical. This will minimise the effects of uneven landing gear forces during these two critical flight phases. In the past, some designers have chosen to arrange the landing gear so that the shaft had some forward tilt on the ground. This helps in forward taxiing but hurts when aerodynamically braking a ground roll or taxiing rearward. High fatigue loads in the main rotor of the Sikorsky UH-60A Black Hawk, which has a 3° forward tilt on the ground, have been attributed to these two manoeuvres.

*Examples of Allowable Flare Angles.* **(Pilot Press)**

## The Landing Gear

Even though the helicopter is a flying machine, a major concern for the designer is how to make it compatible with the ground. There are several options for the landing gear. Most small helicopters, are equipped with skid landing gear. These are simple, easy to maintain, and provide a very stable and positive ground contact that helps in operation from sloping surfaces. Skids can easily be equipped with floats or 'bear feet' for operation from water or from soft sites, and are a convenient place to strap external loads. Ground handling, however, becomes a problem. A helicopter equipped with skids must move from one spot to another either by air-taxiing, by using special ground handling wheels, or by being carried by a dolly. The larger the helicopter, the more difficult it is to handle on skids. For this reason, most large helicopters have wheels. This makes it possible to ground-taxi like an aeroplane using collective pitch to generate thrust and some cyclic pitch to tilt the rotor forward (or even backwards). Ground-taxiing in this manner produces much less rotor downwash than air-taxiing and less danger of blowing over other aircraft parked along the taxi way, less debris blown around, and better visibility if there is dust or snow on the ground.

Wheels also have obvious advantages in rolling takeoffs and landings. It is significant that builders of large helicopters have used wheels from the start whereas builders of small helicopters have generally equipped their aircraft with skids. Bell for its medium helicopters, the 222 and the 214ST, now give the customer the option of taking delivery either with wheels or with skids.

*The Bell 222 with Optional Gear (either with retracting wheels or with skids)*

*Wheel arrangements on the Mi10, H19, Agusta 109
and Agusta 129.*

*Long stroke wheels of the Mi-10 'Harke'.*

*Four-point Sikorsky H-19 arrangement.*

*Retractable Agusta A109 MkII undercarriage.*

*High crashworthy wheels of Agusta 129 Mangusta.*

If the designer wants his helicopter to fly fast, he will consider retracting the landing gear. Wheels lend themselves to this better than skids although several prototype helicopters have had retracting skids. Retractible gear reduces drag but at a price. Non-retractible gear is lighter, simpler, and is more foolproof. It provides more energy absorbtion capability in a crash in which a retractible gear might not be extended. Consequently, helicopter designers still find difficulty in deciding between the advantages of each type.

Most skid gears look about the same but wheels can be arranged in several ways. Heavy-lift helicopters, for example, use four wheels to simplify loading but most others use only three in either a nose-wheel or tail-wheel configuration.

Sometimes special requirements dictate the wheel placement. Sikorsky had equipped the US Army's UH-60A with a sturdy far-aft tail-wheel. This has the advantage of giving the pilot the confidence to make a high nose-up quick stop close to the ground knowing that the tail wheel will protect the back end. When the aircraft was redesigned for the US Navy's Seahawk programme, the tail wheel had to be moved forward so the tail boom could be folded to allow for storage in small warship hangars.

Regardless of the landing gear configuration, engineers must still consider the helicopter's stability while on a hillside or a rolling deck. US Army requirements usually specify the ability to operate on a 15° slope. Such a requirement dictates the location of both the longitudinal and lateral positions of the wheels with respect to the aircraft's centre of gravity.

Tyre sizes are selected based on the need for

*Tail Wheel Placement on the Sikorsky Black Hawk (left) and Seahawk to make latter capable with warship flight decks.*

'flotation' on whatever type of terrain the customer specifies and for the maximum load they must carry. If the helicopter is always expected to operate from hard, solid surfaces such as the deck of a ship, the tyres can be small, such as on the Kaman HU-2, but if it is expected to operate from soft, rain-soaked ground, the tyres must be large. The customer will usually quantify the requirement by specifying the minimum California Bearing Rating (CBR) on which the helicopter must be towed. This can be converted into a maximum pressure per sq in (or sq cm) for the tyre's footprint and used to select the tyre size and pressure.

## Engine Placement

Turboshaft engines are approximately cylindrical in shape so they readily adapt to compact and streamline installations. Most Soviet helicopter engines are designed to be installed ahead of the transmission and their drive shafts therefore come out of the rear. Most modern turboshaft engines developed in the West are front-drive devices that are meant to be installed behind the transmission. Thus by choosing a specific engine, the designer is committed to either a fore or an aft placement unless he is prepared to develop an unorthodox drive train.

With two or more engines, the designer of a commercial helicopter will usually place them close together in the interest of saving weight. Indeed, some like the Pratt & Whitney Canada PT6T-3 'Twin Pac' come already packaged compactly together with a combining gearbox. If he is designing a military helicopter, however, he will place them far apart in the interest of reducing vulnerability.

Intakes should be as high as is practical to reduce the chance of sucking up foreign objects. If the engine does not have an integral particle separator to clean the air of sand and dust, the airframe designer will be expected to provide one! The exhaust system should incorporate an infra-red (IR) suppressor that cools the gasses and shields the hot parts of the engine from direct view of an IR-guided missile. Even after cooling, the gasses should be discharged away from structure and with enough velocity that they are not reingested during prolonged hover.

## The Field-of-View

One of the most important design considerations for a combat helicopter will be to give the crew the best field-of-view possible since a threat can come from any direction. The ideal is to place each member of the crew into a compartment as nearly like a glass sphere as possible. Practical considerations, of course, lead to a design quite inferior to this ideal. For one thing, the designer is faced with the dilemma that transparent panels are difficult to make bullet-proof without large weight penalties. For this reason, the designer would like to keep the transparencies as small as possible even though he knows that for the field-of-view the pilot would like to see them as big as possible. Side panels usually have compound curvature to maximise panel stiffness for low weight and to enhance the 'look about' capability of the crew. The front-facing windscreens have an additional requirement in that they must resist the abrasive action of windshield wipers. On the AH-64A this is achieved by using glass as the outer layer.

Since it is impractical to make the transparencies bullet-proof, in the interest of invulnerability their size is kept to a minimum and armour-plating is installed below their sills. Some designers looking into the future even see a fully armoured cockpit with no transparencies and the pilot relying on television screens for his view of the outside. Another consideration in designing the transparencies is that large areas turn the cockpit into a 'greenhouse' on a sunny day and make the design of an adequate air-conditioning system that much more difficult.

Once the designer has sized the transparencies, he should minimise the restriction of the field-of-view with such things as circuit breaker panels, and large canopy posts.

Designers of attack helicopters with a two-man crew arranged in tandem must decide which seat to give to the pilot and which to give to the co-pilot/gunner. Both have a strong claim to the front seat with the best field-of-view. Designers have generally put the pilot in the back seat although Bell in the YAH-63 did not. One of the rationales for the usual choice is that the position closer to the centre of gravity gives the pilot a better feel when manoeuvreing the aircraft. In some designs, the fact that the weapon sight is in the nose is given as the reason to put the gunner there. In any case the rear seat will be elevated above the front seat to give the second person the best possible view.

The widely-spaced engines that are so desirable for reduced vulnerability decrease the over-the-shoulder visibility. For air-to-air combat, the

*The OH-58D with Hub-Mounted Sight.*

pilot should at least have a rear-view mirror or a rear-facing television camera. Another consideration is that a view of the ground through 'chin windows' just under the pilot's feet is very beneficial for precise flight in the nap-of-the-earth but may be difficult to provide because of the neccessity to install equipment in that particular area.

If the view from the cockpit is not as good as it could be, or if it is desirable to mask as much of the helicopter as possible, a sight mounted on the cabin roof or above the rotor will be considered. A case where the perceived advantages outweighed the disadvantages of drag, weight, and cost is the Bell OH-58D Aeroscout which has a mast-mounted sight.

### Field-of-Fire

If an aircraft is equipped with a turreted weapon, it is desirable to be able to fire it in as wide a range of elevation and azimuth as possible. Bombers in the Second World War accomplished this by using as many as six turrets to cover the entire spherical aspect. Most combat helicopters will probably have only a nose-or belly-mounted gun that will primarily be able to fire in a forward azimuth and elevation. Even if placed right on the nose, the upward field-of fire may be restricted by the rotor disc. It is true, of course, that a similar problem was solved in the First World War by using an interrupter that allowed machine guns to fire through the propeller. Since

a rotor generally has even less solidity than a propeller, it seems reasonable that a similar solution could be developed for the helicopter.

Rockets and missiles are usually fired forward, but there is a desire to have some flexibility in the elevation of launch. This is especially desirable when firing from a hover position to adjust for the relative height of the target or to obtain the maximum range from unguided rockets. This is accomplished on the AH-64 by installing actuators in the wing-mounted racks that can change the elevation ±5°.

## The Inboard Profile Drawing

### Balance

One of the primary features of the inboard profile drawing will be to show the location of the main weight components; such as the crew, payload, engines, landing gear, weapons, fuel tanks, etc. The object will be to locate these so that the aircraft's centre of gravity (CG) will remain on or near the main rotor shaft no matter how the aircraft is loaded. A plot of the extreme centre of gravity position as a function of gross weight as various expendable weights are loaded is known colloquially as the CG 'potato' and was discussed in the chapter on The Preliminary Design Process.

The most aft limit is usually established by the stability and control engineer who knows that as the centre of gravity drifts aft, the manoeuvre stability decreases. Loading the helicopter to the forward limit does not hurt stability but could produce high loads in the rotor and might make it difficult to do a aggressive nose-up flare for a quick-stop. It is true, however, that it is usually very difficult to load a helicopter such that the forward limit is approached. This is partially because even though the designers had good intentions for keeping the centre of gravity forward during the design, more weight is likely to be added to the aft portion during subsequent development than to the front and as a consequence, most actual helicopters have an aft CG problem.

Because a helicopter is relatively symmetrical laterally, the centre of gravity will normally be close to the vertical plane of symmetry. Exceptions that require investigation, however, are those helicopters with heavy expendable wing loads that might become unbalanced due to malfunctions such as the inadvertant jettisoning of one full external fuel tank or the firing of all the missiles from one side but not the other. For these, the designer must insure that the lateral cyclic pitch range is adequate to trim out the offset centre of gravity and that the structure can take the resulting loads.

## Structure

The Inboard Profile Drawing will also show the major structural arrangement. The goal of the structures designer is to provide strength where it is needed and lightness where it is possible. Secondary goals are to design such that manufacturing, maintenance, and repair are as straightforward and easy as possible.

*The Hughes OH-6A*

The first step is to lay out load paths between those components from which loads will originate in flight, in landing, and in a crash. Short and direct load paths connecting the rotor, the engine, the transmission, the fuel tanks, the landing gear, the empennage, the payload or weapons, and the aircraft's centre of gravity are required to minimise structural weight. In laying out the structure, consideration must be given to providing the crew and passengers with adequate 'living room' in a crash in as many different impact conditions as possible. One example of careful design in this regard is given by the arrangement of the McDonnell Douglas MD500 where an A-frame structure joins the primary components.

In addition, the structure and seats supporting the crew and passengers must be designed to absorb energy as they deform to reduce the inertia loads to survivable levels in the acceleration or contact velocity conditions specified by the customer. To ensure survival, the seat and shoulder harnesses must have adequate strength and suitable attachments to the structure so as to restrain the occupants from being thrown into solid objects and every piece of potentially loose equipment must be fastened down so that it does not become a flying projectile.

To ease manufacturing and crash repair, some of the structure is usually designed to be made in distinct components. For example, it is common to design a 'manufacturing joint' to connect the tail boom to the fuselage even though such a break is a weight penalty. For naval helicopters, such a joint may be dictated by the requirement

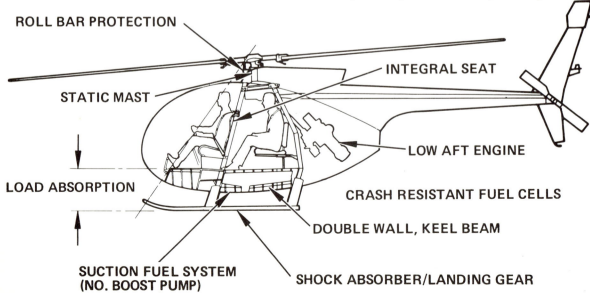

ROLL BAR PROTECTION

INTEGRAL SEAT

STATIC MAST

LOW AFT ENGINE

LOAD ABSORPTION

CRASH RESISTANT FUEL CELLS

DOUBLE WALL, KEEL BEAM

SUCTION FUEL SYSTEM
(NO. BOOST PUMP)

SHOCK ABSORBER/LANDING GEAR

*The McDonnell Douglas AH-64 Fuselage Structure
with work panels folded back.*

to fold the tail boom back parallel to the fuselage
in order to minimise storage problems.

Provisions for easy maintenance was a prime
consideration in the design of the Apache where
major components were attached to a strong
structural deck that when uncovered by folding
back two hinged panels became a work platform
with access to most of the power plant and
control system elements.

## Choice of Structural Materials

The usual structural material of helicopter construction since the Second World War has been
riveted sheet aluminum; and it still is the most
cost effective and satisfactory material for many
applications such as tail booms requiring only
single curvature surfaces. Other metals are used
in special situations where their special charac-

teristics are beneficial. Titanium and stainless
steel are used in rotor hubs and engine compartment firewalls to take advantage of their high
strength and/or high temperature characteristics.
Because of its light weight, magnesium is used
extensively for wheels and cast gear box housings
except on naval helicopters where its poor
corrosion resistance in the presence of salt water
makes it unsuitable. Nickel has an application
for the anti-erosion strip on the blades.

Since about 1960, new materials made up of
very strong fibres of one sort or another firmly
fixed in an organic 'matrix' and known as
'composites' have been finding more and more
applications. Their attractions come primarily by
combining high strength and rigidity with low
weight and the capability of being readily
formed in a variety of complicated shapes.
Compared to metals, they are corrosion-free and
have high resistance to fatigue. In many components, their use eliminates assembly details,
reduces complexity and lowers manufacturing

costs. For some applications, they have greater damage tolerance than metals, are more survivable against combat damage and can be repaired in the field more easily.

Against these advantages are a number of disadvantages. Although strong in tension, composites are generally weak in compression which makes fastening parts together with conventional fasteners such as bolts and rivets difficult. (It has been said that composites are like a mass of fishhooks – resistant to being pulled apart, but collapsing readily when pushed together). Because of their organic matrix, they tend to be sensitive to temperature, ultra-violet radiation and lightning strikes since they are poor conductors of electricity (and of heat). Edges must be sealed to prevent the entry of moisture that might freeze and split the plys. They have poor erosion resistance and many are very brittle. Finally, the cost is high; not only for the material itself, but for the tooling and testing required to assure good quality. Despite these negatives, in many applications the composite advantages are overwhelming enough to ensure their use.

Composites were first used in the form of fibreglass in non-structural components such as aerodynamic fairings and access doors. One of their primary attributes for these applications is the ease of forming parts with compound curvature compared to using sheet aluminum. The first structural components made of composites were fibreglass rotor blades pioneered by MBB in West Germany in the early 1960s. Rotor blades are primarily loaded in tension by centrifugal forces and the good characteristics of composites in this application could be taken advantage of. For rotor blades, composites provide little weight benefit since the rotor moment of inertia and thus the weight is almost always dictated by the autorotational requirement, but the good fatigue life of the fiberglass (similar to wood) allowed the designers to guarantee much longer fatigue lives than they had been able to do with their previous metal blades.

Since composite leading edges do not have good erosion resistance, they are usually covered with a metal protective strip of thin titanium or nickel sheet. This is done at the expense of the otherwise low radar signal returned from composite blades. If a de-icing system is installed, it is as an electrical heating blanket under the erosion strip.

Composites generally fail gradually and this failure is signalled by visual clues such as crazing of the surface epoxy or the appearance of frayed filaments. To take full advantage of this feature, both sides of a composite structure should be open to inspection. This is a requirement of the US Navy that precludes the use of closed components that would otherwise be lighter.

The development of more advanced (and costly) filament materials such as boron and graphite and the organic material, Kevlar, has allowed designers to consider these for other structural components such as the airframe, the rotor hub, the swashplate, the tail rotor drive shaft, gearbox housings, and even the landing gear.

Two further developments of composites may have advantages for use in the future: thermoplastic composites and metal matrix composites. Most of the organic matrix composites are formed at room temperature by applying liquid epoxy to layers of fabric and then are 'set' at some higher temperature while being pressurised in a tool for several hours. These are 'thermosetting' composites. Another type is the 'thermoplastic' composite which promises high toughness and can be formed in minutes but the tools must be heated to as high as 800°F (426°C).

Composites using metal instead of epoxy for the matrix hold promise for applications in which high temperature or high compressive strength is needed.

# Component Systems

## Control Systems

The main and tail rotors are magnificent manoeuvreing devices but they must be made to do what the pilot wants. That is the job of the control system. Most single rotor helicopters use the basic control system shown below.

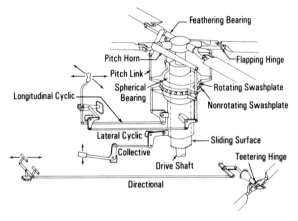

*Basic Control System*

This system consists of three sub-systems: main rotor collective, main rotor cyclic, and directional (tail rotor).

### The Collective System

The function of the main rotor collective is to vary the amount of thrust the rotor produces and to compensate for the inflow through the rotor in both hover and forward flight. This is done by simultaneously changing the pitch of all of the blades by the same amount in response to an up-and-down motion of the collective pitch stick in the pilot's left hand.

### The Cyclic System

The cyclic system was originally developed for autogiros. It controls the direction of thrust by causing the rotor disc to tilt with respect to the shaft in response to fore-and-aft or side-to-side motion of the cyclic stick in the pilot's right hand. When the stick is moved, the control linkages act on the swashplate which is free to tilt in any direction about a large spherical bearing or a set of gimbals. The swashplate consists of two parts: a non-rotating lower half connected to the control linkages from the cockpit and a rotating upper half that follows the motion of the non-rotating swashplate through a set of bearings.

From the rotating swashplate, the motion goes up to a pitch horn on each blade, causing the blade pitch to be changed around a feathering bearing or a torsionally soft structural component. (In practice, the pitch horns are not made as long as drawn. By reorienting the non-rotating swashplate clockwise, the same effect can be obtained with shorter pitch horns). When the stick is pushed forward, the blade on the right side has its pitch reduced, whereas the blade on the left has its pitch increased by the same amount. Thus the pitch of each blade changes 'cyclically' or once every revolution. Cyclic pitch has two functions: it changes the angle of attack on the two sides of the rotor to make up for the asymmetry of air velocity to keep the rotor trimmed in forward flight, and it allows the pilot to start a manoeuvre using rotor flapping by deliberately unbalancing the lift. For example, from a trim condition, if the pilot pushes forward on the cyclic stick, the rotor will respond a quarter of a revolution later by flapping down in front thus applying a nose-down pitching moment to the aircraft. Rolling moments are produced by making the rotor disc tilt to the side so that the direction of its thrust vector follows the orientation of the cyclic stick.

One alternative to the swashplate is the spider system used on some Westland designs as shown below.

Another alternative is the system used on Kaman helicopters. With this system, both collective and cyclic control are obtained by

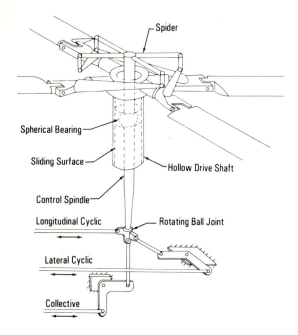

*The Westland Spider System*

twisting flexible blades by the forces from controllable 'servoflaps' fixed to the trailing edge.

When the trailing edge of the servoflap goes up, it produces a download at the blade's trailing edge and twists the blade nose- up.

## Directional Control

The control system for the tail rotor is a collective system just as on the main rotor. The

*The Kaman Servoflap System*

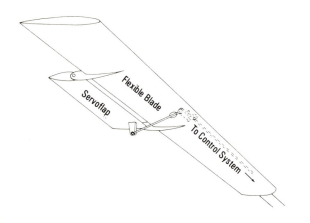

pilot uses it to control the thrust of the tail rotor but has no control over its flapping which is allowed to find its own equilibrium position as affected by flight conditions. The control is by 'rudder pedals' rigged like an aeroplane's – to produce a right turn when the right pedal is pressed.

## Hydraulic Control Systems

A simple control system not only transmits signals from the cockpit to the rotors, but also allows forces generated at the rotors to be transmitted back to the cockpit. For small helicopters, these control forces are relatively light and can be made manageable with such things as adjustable springs and friction devices that allow the pilot to relieve steady control loads and to at least momentarily release a control to tune a radio or handle a map. On larger helicopters, however, the sizeable aero-dynamic and dynamic loads generated at the rotor and fed back through the control system are too large to be compensated for with simple devices. For these, the helicopter designers have followed the lead of the aeroplane designers and have used hydraulic actuators to provide the

*Details of a Hydraulic Control System*

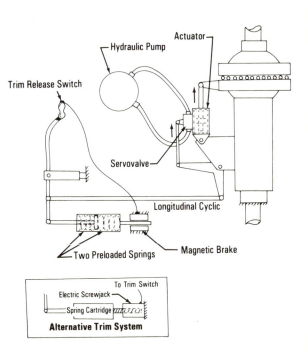

muscle while intercepting the rotor loads and grounding them to the structure near the main or tail rotor support assemblies before they get to the cockpit.

Moderately-sized helicopters can be satisfactory flown with only one hydraulic system since even with it turned off, the pilot can fly the helicopter (although with great difficulty, to be sure). For this purpose, each actuator contains a by-pass valve that opens when the hydraulic pressure fails. Larger helicopters have two or more independent hydraulic systems to make sure that one is always working.

## Control Feel

With irreversible control actuators, the pilot is only moving low-friction servovalves with his cockpit controls. He gets no feel from control motion and if he were to release a control, it might fall over due to its own weight. To remedy this situation, control centering and artificial feel are built into the cyclic control system and sometimes into the directional as well whereas the collective system is usually equipped only with an adjustable friction device and if necessary a helper spring to balance the weight of the control rods between the cockpit and the collective actuator.

Although pilots differ in what they consider to be optimum control feel, most modern helicopters with a floor-mounted cyclic stick have a longitudinal force gradient of 1 to 4 lb/in (0.2 to 0.7 kg/cm), with the lateral system being somewhat less. This is in recognition of the relative strength of the arm in the two directions and is part of what is called 'control harmony'. In addition to the gradient, the control should have a definite 'detent' position that requires some force to initially move or to 'breakout' the control. The detent effect can be achieved by pre-loading two springs against each other in a cartridge in a control rod. The gradient and the detent insure that the control will stay put if the pilot lets it go momentarily and it gives him a tactile reference to return to after a manoeuvre.

## Trim Systems

A change in flight condition also requires a change in the position of the cyclic control. To relieve the control forces, it is necessary to re-orient the detent to the new trim point. There are two types of trim systems on modern helicopters. On one, a magnetic brake is used to fix the anchor point of the feel spring to structure. The magnetic brake freezes when its electricity is shut off. When the pilot pushes the button on his cyclic stick, he electrifies the material in the brake, causing it to 'thaw' and allowing the springs to quickly reset themselves to their new zero-force point. The other trim system uses an electric motor and a screw jack to relatively slowly adjust the spring's anchor point in response to a four-way 'coolie-hat' switch on the top of the cyclic stick. There is no consensus as to which is the best system; some designers have included both.

In addition to a spring force gradient on pedals, Sikorsky designers include a damper in the directional control system that produces a force as a function of the speed with which the pilot moves the pedals. This alleviates the danger of over-torquing the tail rotor drive system by stalling the tail rotor when rapidly recovering from a right hovering turn when more pitch might be demanded than is compatible with the instantaneous flow field.

Because of the geometry and the weight of the control system between the cockpit and the actuators, extraneous control forces might be generated in manoeuvres where the G forces acting on the control rods will produce forces at the stick or pedals. To prevent this, several helicopter design teams have found it desirable to mass balance the control system with strategically located weights.

Even though it takes only a small amount of force to move the actuator servovalves, the writers of military specifications insist on stout control systems between the cockpit and the actuators. This is because someone getting in and out of the cockpit might inadvertently put high loads on the sticks or pedals. Another reason is that control systems occasionally get jammed by battle damage or by foreign objects. The system should be robust enough to clear a jam with all the effort the pilot can exert.

## Stability and Control Augmentation Systems

Once hydraulic actuators have been introduced into the control system, it is relatively easy to add gyros or other sophisticated devices to make flying easier and safer.

Although mechanical components were originally employed, the current practice is to use devices emitting electrical signals. These signals can be sent directly to a Stability and

Command Augmentation System (SCAS) computer and then to an electrically powered servovalve that moves the actuator independently of the pilot.

Typical of these systems is the one used on the AH-64 showing the following schematic.

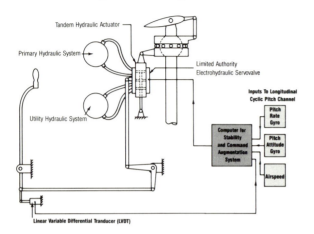

*Dual Hydraulic System and SCAS*

In this system – typical of 1975 design technology – the servovalve controlled by the pilot can move the actuator from fully contracted to fully extended. The electrohydraulic valve controlled by the SCAS computer, on the other hand, is limited to only 10 per cent of full stroke on each side of the pilot's command. This prevents an error in a sensor or in the computer from producing an uncommanded full-stroke actuator hardover. Even the effect of a 10 per cent hardover is minimised by monitoring the SCAS and immediately nulling its command if it is detected doing something uncalled for by the system.

One type of signal going to the computer is from the linear variable differential transducer (LVDT) attached to each cockpit control. These signals improve controllability by overriding the gyro-stabilising signals that would normally fight the pilot during manoeuvres. This signal can also be used by the computer to 'shape' the control input to the actuator by either speeding it up or slowing it down to better tailor the controllability to what pilots desire.

## Fly-by-Wire

The presence of these LVDT's leads to the possibility of using electric signals in place of mechanical motions to control the actuators in what has become to be known as a 'fly-by-wire' system. In the AH-64, this possibility has been used to create a back-up control system (BUCS) to take over in case of battle damage. If the mechanical system is severed, BUCS is immediately activated using the LVDT in the severed channel and giving it full authority over the appropriate actuator. If the mechanical control system is jammed rather than severed, the pilot can go to BUCS by exerting enough force to break a shear pin. By design, when the AH-64 is flying on BUCS, the affected channel accepts only signals from the pilot's control and none from the gyros or airspeed sensors. The reason for this is that the helicopter is now flying on a 'single thread' and the designers did not want any other possible failures to jeopardise the remainder of the flight for which the pilot is advised to quickly finish what he is doing and head home for repairs.

The AH-64 BUCS concept can be used as the basis for a full fly-by-wire system by not including the push-pull tubes, bellcranks, and cables between the cockpit and the actuators. Now reliability becomes a major design consideration, since jeopardising the aircraft with any single failure is not permissible. This is usually handled by using triply – or even quadruply – redundant independent channels with some sort of 'voting' so that any channel that is not tracking the others can be switched off.

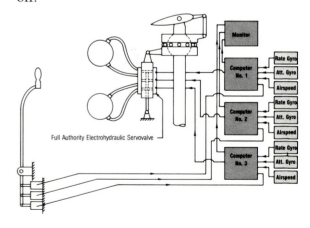

*Triply Redundant Fly-By-Wire System*

This redundancy gives the control system 'fail-safe' capability; that is, its performance is not degraded by a single failure. Especially for combat helicopters, physical separation of the wires and the various elements of the system is very important to avoid a single hit from destroying more than one of the vital components.

There is obviously a weight saving achieved by eliminating the mechanical elements, but the necessity of adding redundancy in the electronic components at least partially reduces the savings, and of course adds to the cost of the helicopter.

## Fly-by-Light

Fly-by-wire can do everything the designer wants but it might also do something he does not want. During a thunderstorm, the wires might act as antennae and generate transient electrical spikes in response to lightning strikes or even near misses. These could be interpreted by the system as true control commands leading to out-of-control flying. To protect against this, inventors have developed 'fly-by-light' systems in which a coded series of light pulses travelling through optic fibre cables carries the information from

*Installation of a Side-Arm Controller simplifies the cockpit area and gives a better view of the instrument panel.*

the cockpit and other sensors to the computers and then to the actuators.

## Side-Arm Controllers

The next generation of helicopters may have a different cockpit arrangement than the present systems with their floor-mounted controls. With fly-by-wire or by light, it is feasible to place all of the control functions in one 'manipulator', usually known as a 'side-arm controller' that will simplify the cockpit while giving a better view of the instrument panel. Collective can be obtained with up and down forces, cyclic with longitudinal and lateral forces, and directional with rotation.

Prototypes of this type of controller have little or no motion but electrically sense forces being applied by the pilot's hand and send the signal over wires or optic cables directly to the actuators. At this writing, there is no consensus as to what levels of force are optimum or even whether it is desirable to put all four controls on the same manipulator. Some pilots who have flown prototypes of these systems prefer to keep the collective on the conventional lever because its strong position clue correlates with engine

power which is always of interest.

Special considerations that arise when side-arm controllers are contemplated are the necessity on combat aircraft to provide both right and left controllers to anticipate an arm wound and the logic to be used in two-pilot aircraft to insure that only one is in control of the aircraft at any one time.

## Advanced Concepts

Although the control systems used on current helicopters can be rated as generally satisfactory, it has been recognised for some time that improvements could make the pilot's task easier, especially in such high work-load situations as combat. Most man-carrying vehicles have controls that the operator manipulates to achieve some desired rate of linear or angular velocity. For example, an automobile's accelerator governs forward speed and it's steering wheel the rate of turn. The characteristic of a rate system is that a velocity is established by moving the control and then stopped by moving it back to its original position. An attitude control system, on the other hand, changes either attitude or distance proportional to the displacement of the manipulator with no subsequent need to change the control. The classic example of an attitude control is the self-service elevator that requires only one push of a button to deliver you to the desired floor.

In and near hover, the control systems of current helicopters do a pretty good job of being rate systems. One of the best in this regard is the main rotor collective pitch. An increase in this control causes the helicopter to rapidly accelerate upward until a steady rate of climb is established. The climb is stopped by returning the control to its original position. A tail rotor operates similarly to a main rotor: a change in its collective pitch will result in a hover turn at a constant rate that is stopped by returning the pedals to their original setting.

Even cyclic pitch is a rate control in and near hover. For example, a forward cyclic control input causes the rotor to precess nose-down as a gyroscope so that its pitch rate – at least initially – is proportional to the longitudinal control displacement. After a few seconds, however, this changes the tilt of the rotor and causes the helicopter to translate into forward flight.

With forward flight comes asymmetric aerodynamics. These produce nose-up flapping that eventually stops the angular rate and leaves the helicopter tilted nose-down and accelerating forward. Eventually, even this vanishes leaving the helicopter tilted nose-down in steady forward flight at some speed proportional to the longitudinal cyclic pitch. Thus the cyclic pitch may be considered to be a rate system on pitch attitude for a short-time response, but an attitude system in the long run. At the same time, the cyclic is a short-time acceleration control for translational motion, changing to a rate system in that it eventually results in a new trim speed.

In none of these responses is the result entirely satisfactory to the pilot or to the flying qualities engineer, in that the helicopter is slow to settle down and usually goes through some unwanted overshoots unless restrained by the pilot. In addition, almost all control inputs generate nuisance cross-coupling responses in other axes. The addition of a sophisticated stability and control augmentation system using a computer and suitable sensors can markedly improve the flying qualities by making the response 'crisper' and by minimising the cross-coupling and can even be used to change one type of response to another in various situations.

Helicopter test flying and simulation studies with various types of 'control laws' have shown that rate control system are preferable for rapid manoeuvres requiring gross changes in flight path or airspeed but attitude systems are preferable when only small changes are required. The proper sensors and programs in the SCAS computer can make the change either automatically or at the pilot's command. A control system which includes all of the desired capabilities is referred to as being 'highly augmented'.

These systems often use a 'model following' scheme in which the computer is programmed with the equations of motion of an ideal helicopter that responds to the pilot's commands and to the outside environment as sensed by various instruments. Then, the actual helicopter looks at what the computer model is doing and imitates it in a follow-the-leader mode. Of course, this works best if the capabilities of the manoeuvreing computer model are limited to what the actual helicopter can physically do. Another consideration of this approach is that assurance must be provided that no failure of a sensor measuring airspeed, groundspeed, ground position, altitude, heading, or other parameter will induce an unwanted control motion. For this reason, most of these sensors must be duplicated or even triplicated to insure flight safety.

Since the desired flight characteristics are

different at low speed than at high, the designer may choose to use an airspeed or a groundspeed signal to change the control laws. He also will probably find it desirable to switch control laws when the helicopter is on the ground using a 'squat switch' to sense oleo compression. At high speed, he may choose to retain the basic helicopter's characteristics, only using augmentation to smooth the rough edges. This is done by stabilisation, response quickening, increasing damping, minimising cross-coupling, providing pedal-fixed turn coordination, and providing the option to hold altitude, speed, and compass heading in unattended flight while the pilot does such attention-diverting tasks as reading maps and tuning radios.

At low speed, turn coordination is neither necessary nor even desirable, so this would be phased out at speeds below 20 to 40 kts (37 to 74 km/h). Instead, for precision hovering, lateral cyclic pitch should control either sideward velocity or sideward displacement with the longitudinal pitch doing the same in its axis. In this speed regime, also, altitude control should probably be based on radar altitude rather than barometric altitude as would be satisfactory in most high speed conditions.

Once given the flexibilty of a model-following scheme, the designer can introduce some very fundamental changes into the way a helicopter is flown. One suggested modification involves separating the functions of the collective and longitudinal cyclic pitch controls in forward flight. In a conventional helicopter, the pilot must use a combination of collective and cyclic to change either airspeed or rate-of-climb without affecting the other. With suitable control laws enforced by a highly-augmented control system, the designer can make the collective manipulator control only rate-of-climb as it does in hover, while longitudinal cyclic controls only airspeed without changing altitude. Whether this or other major changes are desirable can be evaluated using a test helicopter equipped with a reprogrammable flight computer.

# The Power Train

The design problem of transmitting the power from the engine to the rotors of a helicopter is almost the same as that of transmitting the power from the engine to the wheels of an automobile. In a sense, the helicopter problem is simpler since no shifting of gears must be provided for. On the other hand, the helicopter transmission designer, unlike the automobile designer, must continually bear in mind how important weight is to his vehicle and how safety-of-flight depends on the continuing operation of his transmission. Another factor is that the development of a new automobile transmission is generally an evolutionary process carried out over a period of years building on the experience of literally millions of similar transmissions, whereas the designer of the helicopter transmission must often start out almost from scratch.

## Speed Reduction

In all cases, the transmission must reduce the rotational speed from thousands of revolutions per minute at the engine shaft to hundreds of revolutions per minute at the main rotor. To do this, the drive train must have gear reductions ratios in the neighbourhood of ten-to-one for reciprocating engines and as high as a hundred-to-one for large helicopters powered with turbine engines.

One of the first decisions for the transmission designer is the number of stages of reduction to be used to obtain the overall gear ratio. Current designers generally opt for either three or four stages. They have several choices available for the type of gearing in each stage. One is a spiral bevel gear set which is especially convenient if it is required to transmit the power through an angle. The second is the helical gear, and the third, the planetary.

As a rule-of-thumb, the planetary is the lightest, the helical gear weighs about twice as much and the spiral bevel gear about four times as much.

It may be educational to look at two design approaches for the same type of helicopter that resulted in quite different hardware. In 1973, the US Army selected both Bell and Hughes to develop competing versions of the Advanced Attack Helicopter (AAH) using two of the then new General Electric T700 turboshafts. These engines had an output speed of 20000 rpm and were to drive a main rotor turning at less than 300 rpm. Because of the high priority for invulnerability, each team designed their aircraft with the engines as widely apart as possible without jeopardising the ability to be transported in a Lockheed C-130 transport aircraft.

For the YAH-63, Bell chose to use one stage

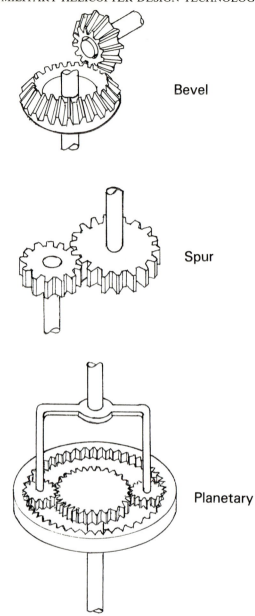

**Bevel**

**Spur**

**Planetary**

*Gear Configurations*

of bevel gears and two of helical gears in what they called a 'Flat Pack' transmission.

The two engines drove directly into the transmission through the spiral bevel gears.

Hughes, taking a somewhat different approach, used four stages. The first was a bevel gear set in a separate engine nose gearbox that reduced the rotational speed by more than half. Inside the main transmission, was one bevel set, one spur set, and one planetary set to achieve the rest of the reduction.

Each design team cited different reasons for making their choices. Bell pointed out that with their design, the intermediate nose gearboxes were not required. They therefore achieved simplicity, compactness, and light weight. Hughes argued that with their design, by including flexible couplings between the nose gearbox and the main transmission, engine alignment would not be as critical and that by using slower speeds inside the transmission, the capability of bearings to survive after failure of the lubrication system would be enhanced.

Subsequent development and flying of the two designs showed that the Bell selection had been unfortunate in that the rigid interface between the engines and the transmission required extremely accurate alignment procedures to assure an adequate engine life. The replacement of many damaged engines on the YAH-63 during the competive evaluation was a decisive factor in the selection by the US Army of the Hughes YAH-64 for the production contract.

All transmission designers include an overrunning clutch between the engine and the transmission so that the rotor can freely turn even after an engine stops. In all cases, the tail rotor is driven directly from the main rotor transmission so that directional control is not lost in autorotation. This applies even to the NOTAR concept where the fan supplying air to the tail boom is driven from the main rotor transmission.

Most helicopters use a rotating main rotor shaft in which the torque, the lifting force, and rotor pitch and roll moments are all carried from the rotor hub to the transmission case and then to the fuselage. The Hughes/McDonnell Douglas designers, on the other hand, have opted for a 'static mast' concept in which a non-rotating, hollow mast supports the rotor hub on a bearing which transmits lift and moments to the airframe while torque is transmitted through a separate rotating drive shaft which contains a shear section that in case of a jammed transmission will fracture at a point that permits the main and tail rotor combination to remain turning for an autorotational landing. This system also allows the static mast to be designed for required pylon bending stiffness and the drive shaft stiffness solely by torsional stiffness requirements. Separation of these requirements allows the designer to tailor the dynamic characteristics in the interests of low vibration without the use of other heavy and complicated solutions.

The scheme has two primary advantages: oscillating, fatigue producing stresses are con-

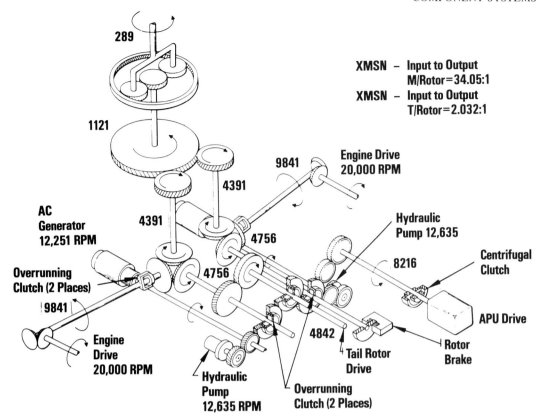

XMSN – Input to Output
M/Rotor=34.05:1

XMSN – Input to Output
T/Rotor=2.032:1

*The AH-64 Transmission*

tained in the non-rotating structure where they are less critical, and the transmission can be changed without disturbing the rotor and the upper control system.

Most large helicopters are equipped with an Auxiliary Propulsion Unit (APU) consisting of a small turbine engine that is primarily used for starting the main engines using compressed air or hydraulic power but which can also drive generators and hydraulic pumps to operate the aircraft systems before starting the main engines.

## Oil or Grease?

The traditional lubrication for helicopter transmissions has been oil but grease is also a viable lubrication. Oil has the advantage that it serves as a good medium for the transfer of heat. It is generally pumped out of the gearbox, passed through an oil cooler, and then sent back in. As it comes out, its temperature gives an indication of the health of the gearbox. A sudden rise in oil temperature warns the pilot of either a low oil supply or of unusual wear in the gears or bearings. The flow of oil also can be passed through filtres to trap any debris and past chip detectors to give another warning of impending trouble. Its disadvantage is that as a fairly low viscosity fluid, it will leak out of any crack or bullet hole, leaving the transmission dry – or nearly so unless the designers have included dams and wicks to provide at least a short-time protection.

*The Static Mast Concept*

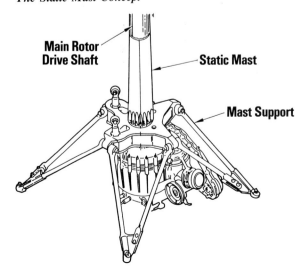

Main Rotor
Drive Shaft

Static Mast

Mast Support

High viscosity grease, on the other hand, will not leak out and so the gearbox will retain adequate lubrication even if damaged. Its disadvantage is that since grease cannot be cycled through a cooler, the gearbox must be designed with other means of heat rejection and with other means of signalling distress. The first is usually taken care of with external fins and some means, such as a fan, to pass air around the box. Strategically placed thermocouples are used to detect incipient bearing and gear tooth failures or a vibration sensor is provided to detect changes in the dynamics that accompany such failures.

On the AH-64, the engine nose gearboxes and the main transmission are oil lubricated, but the two gearboxes in the tail rotor drive system are grease-filled.

## The Tail Rotor Shaft

Horsepower is proportional to the product of torque and rpm. Stresses are proportional to torque and are inversely proportional to the moment of inertia of the shaft. When these relationships are studied together, it becomes evident that to minimise weight it is desirable to

use a large diameter, thin-wall tail rotor drive shaft turning at high speed. The designer, however, is constrained as to how far he can follow this lead. One constraint is the minimum wall thickness that is practical considering that the shafting must be handled during maintenance in the field. Experience has shown that for typically used aluminum tubing, the minimum practical wall thickness for this application is about 0.050 in (1.27 mm).

The other constraint is in selecting the speed of the shaft. A rotating shaft has several unique natural frequencies at which it will develop high whipping displacements due to the centrifugal forces associated with small imbalances. These resonating natural frequencies are functions of the shaft, length stiffness and weight and are referred to as the first, second, third, . . ., critical frequencies. If the shaft is operated on or near one of these, it will not last very long. For that reason, the designer, must trade off the shaft rpm and its stiffness to optimise it with respect to weight. A resonating condition can be controlled with damping. The designers of McDonnell Douglas helicopters have used this to operate their tail rotor drive shafts at 'super-critical' shaft speeds between the first and second critical frequencies. A damper is located near the middle of the shaft to control it while quickly

*The Tail Rotor Drive Configuration on the AH-64*

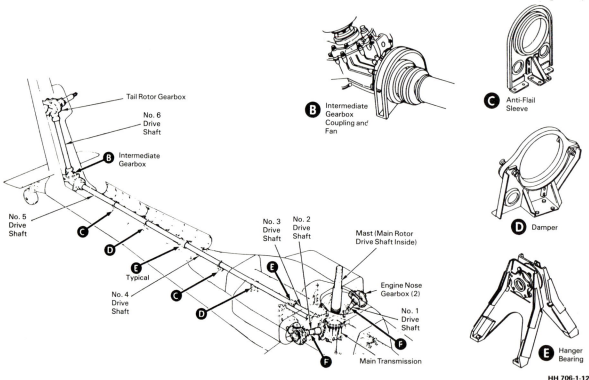

HH 706-1-12

going through the first critical speed – at about 40 per cent of full speed – on the way to full operating speed. This allows them to use a lighter shaft than if it were designed to operate subcritically. To control the shaft in case the damper should suffer combat damage, they install 'anti-flail' devices as shown below.

To allow for some misalignment of the shaft either due to manufacturing inaccuracies or to tail boom deflection under load, flexible couplings are installed at each end.

# The Airspeed System

All helicopters are equipped with a conventional, aeroplane-type airspeed system and some also with a special system intended to accurately measure below the low speed threshold of the conventional system.

The conventional system uses the difference between the 'total' pressure (developed by stopping the air completely) and the 'static' pressure corresponding to that in the air mass before the aircraft approaches. This difference is the 'dynamic' pressure which is proportional to the square of the airspeed. The total pressure is sensed by a forward-facing pitot tube and the static by ports positioned to ignore local airspeed. Both are plumbed to a pressure cell with the total pressure going to the inside and the static to the outside.

As the cell expands due to the pressure difference – the dynamic pressure – it operates

*The Airspeed System on the Mi-24.*

the needle on the face of the indicator.

A challenge for the designer is to find locations for the pitot tube and the static ports that are minimally affected by the downwash of the rotor. During the development flying of a new helicopter, it is usually equipped with a forward-extended instrumentation boom carrying a swivelling pitot-static system that not only measures the airspeed but its direction as well. This test location can then be used to compare with candidate locations on the rest of the helicopter. The Mil design bureau chose to retain the boom position on the Mi-24 and even the swivelling head whose measurements are used in the fire-control system for the gun and rockets.

Other helicopters use fuselage-mounted systems; some of which have been moved from one place to another since the prototype was first flown.

## Low Speed Measurement

A basic problem with the conventional system is that if the pressure cell is strong enough to withstand the dynamic pressure at high speed, it is too stiff to react at low speeds. This is not a problem on aeroplanes which do not fly slowly but it is a problem for helicopters if it is necessary to know accurately the speed and direction of the air in all flight conditions. Several prototype systems have mounted pressure transducers on the blade tips and then processed the sinusoidal signals in a computer to deduce both the airspeed and the direction.

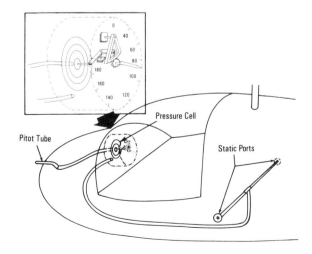

*Typical Airspeed System*

*Airspeed System examples on the Sikorsky S-61, the
Bell 412 and the SA 365N (anti–clockwise).*

Although this system is not used on any production helicopters, a version operates on the AH-64A and the Aerospatiale HH-65A in the form of a small motor-driven beam with a pair of Venturi tubes.

Several other low-speed systems are being used – for instance on tanks – and others are being developed.

*A low-speed airspeed system as demonstrated by the Pacer installation on the HH-65.*

# Designing for Emergencies

Although most of the time the helicopter is flying in routine, trouble-free conditions, it is not always the case. Sometimes a non-routine situation places the helicopter and its occupants in jeopardy. Emergency situations arise from different sources. Some are man-made such as combat damage deliberately inflicted by an opponent or those due to 'pilot error' that result in striking the ground or an obstacle with more velocity than intended. Others come from a caprice of Nature, such as those due to icing, while others are due to some failure in the aircraft as components cease to operate as designed for one reason or another.

For military helicopters, it is up to the customer to anticipate what emergencies must be considered and to what extent they must be met. He should have some knowledge of the cost and weight increases that his requirements impose on the final design since these will have an influence on how many helicopters can be procured on a restricted budget and also on what size the helicopter must be to produce the required performance. It has been aptly said for dilemmas like this: 'The best is the enemy of the good.'

It is the designer's task to provide ways to satisfy the customer's requirements with minimum cost and weight penalties. Now with almost a century of mechanical flight experience behind us, we hopefully know almost everything that can happen to an aircraft and can use the solutions that previous designers have developed to give the pilot the best chance to avoid or to cope with an emergency.

## Minimising Combat Damage

By their very nature, military helicopters are going to be shot at and hit. The designer's ultimate goal is to make his aircraft 'invulnerable', or if that is not possible or practical, to at least provide features that minimise combat damage so that the helicopter can be flown home or landed without injuring the occupants. The features designed into the helicopter will depend on the 'threat' as specified by the procuring agency. The requirement for the Sikorsky Black Hawk and the McDonnell Douglas Apache was that no single 12.7 mm (0.50 in) armour piercing incendiary (API) round could do enough damage that the mission would have to be aborted. In addition, it was desired that the damage due to the Soviet 23 mm high explosive incendiary (HEI) round would do minimum damage. For the first threat, the required 'vulnerable area' was to be zero and for the second threat the minimum possible.

The vulnerable area of the helicopter is determined by examining all of the critical structural elements and components to determine how much damage the specified round would do if it were to impact from any direction whether it is still coming straight or is tumbling. The designer has several basic choices: he can make each critical structural element and component stout enough to 'defeat' the round without impairing its function; he can provide enough material that even with a hole made by a hit, the part will carry the required load; he can locate a critical part so that it is protected by non-critical parts; he can provide 'redundancy' so that if one part is destroyed, another part can take its place; or in the last resort, he can protect a part with parasitic armour. Few of these options come free in terms of weight and/or cost, so the designer must choose very carefully. As an example of how these choices have been implemented on a current combat helicopter, the design options chosen for the McDonnell Douglas AH-64A Apache will be used for illustration.

After weighing the various choices, the designers decided that there were several places on the main and tail rotors and their respective control systems where the only practical option for achieving invulnerability from the specified 12.7 mm threat was to use stout parts. These included the rotor masts (the Hughes design philosophy was to use a non-rotating 'static mast' to support the rotor with the rotating drive shaft inside), the control actuators and the mechanism between them and the swashplate, the swashplate itself, the blade attachments to the hub, and the pitch arms and links. The material chosen for most of these parts was ESR (Electro Slag Remelt) 4340 steel. Because of its purity, this steel can be heat-treated to very high strength while still retaining good toughness.

The two tail rotor gearbox housings are made of high strength aluminum that can also defeat the 12.7 mm round. They are grease-filled so that even if the cases are punctured, they will retain lubrication. The main rotor transmission is oil-lubricated but contains oil dams and wicks that insure that it can transmit full power for at least 30 min following failure of its oil system either through leakage or by failure of both of its oil pumps.

Other parts, such as the tail rotor drive shaft and the structural airframe components, were designed large enough so that even a tumbling 12.7 mm round would leave enough structure to carry the load without failing.

In other places, redundancy was used. The major redundancy was specified by the US Army who wanted a crew of two and twin engines. (This position has not always been consistent. On a previous attack helicopter, the Lockheed Cheyenne, the US Army had specified a single engine, the General Electric T64, and on a subsequent new generation attack helicopter, the

LHX, it at first specified a one-man crew). The two-man Apache cockpit is divided into two separate compartments, one behind the other, with a transparent blast shield between them that can isolate the explosion of a 23 mm HEI round to only one compartment and will also serve as a roll-bar in case the helicopter becomes inverted during a crash.

Each of the crew seats is provided with ceramic armour both in the seat pan and with side pieces. Both cockpits have full flight controls and instruments so that either pilot can fly the aircraft.

The three control actuators for the main rotor and the single actuator for the tail rotor are 'tandem' devices, with two pistons, each actuated by its own separate hydraulic system. The pistons are frangible so if one of them is damaged, it will break into small pieces that will not jam the remaining part of the actuator. The actuator body itself is made of ESR steel to give it high protection against the threat.

A back-up control system (BUCS) was designed to take over the control functions with electric signals between the cockpit and the actuators in case the basic mechanical system was either severed or jammed.

Redundancy was also designed into the blades of the main rotor which have four separate hollow spars and a load-carrying leading edge balance bar. Ballistic tests prove that even

*Protection in the AH-64 Cockpit*

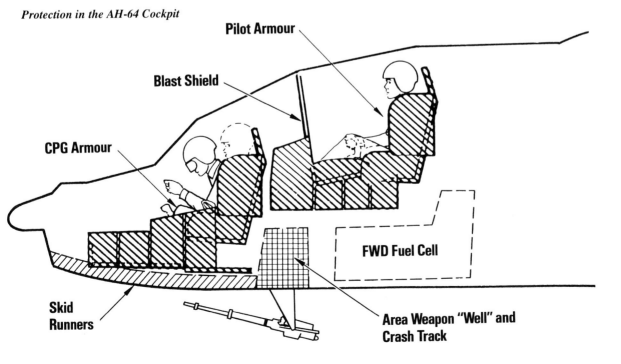

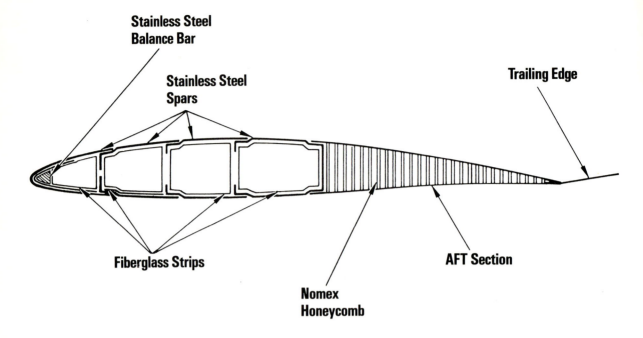

*The Blade Structure, AH-64*

though a 23 mm HEI round leaves a large hole, it does not destroy the load-carrying capability of the blade. If the blade had much less chord than its 21 in (53 cm), no spar redundancy would let it cope with the 8 to 10 in (20 to 25 cm) hole that the 23 mm round makes.

The blades also had to be designed to survive the effects of cutting through a two-inch tree limb.

Two dampers are installed on each blade. Each is strong enough to prevent ground resonance under the worst conditions.

The tail rotor blade has three spars but a chord of only 10 ins (25 cms). As such, it could take a 12.7 mm round but a 23 mm hitting in the right place would destroy it. As discussed earlier, the RFP's for both the UTTAS that later became the UH-60 and the AAH that later became the AH-64 recognised this possibility and required that the aircraft be able to fly home without a tail rotor. Each was originally designed with a large enough vertical stabiliser that at near the forward speed for minimum power and with about 20° of sideslip they could do this. It was discovered, however, during the flight test development phase, that such large vertical stabilisers severely interfered with sideward flight and so on both aircraft, the trailing edge of the vertical fin was modified to reduce its area. As a

consequence, neither helicopter can now meet the original intent of the specification writers. They must descend under partial power, but at time of writing, neither has had a complete tail rotor failure.

The two General Electric T700 engines were placed as far apart as was considered practical in order to minimise the damage that a single round could do.

Redundancy in the fuel system is achieved by using two fuel tanks, each normally feeding a separate engine although with provisions for cross-feeding to either transfer fuel from one tank to the other or for feeding both engines from the same tank.

# Crashworthiness

## Absorbing Energy

In the unfortunate situation in which the helicopter touches down with much more velocity than intended, the designers have to consider means of protecting the occupants. The requirement for the Apache was that they had to be uninjured in a vertical touchdown of 42 ft/s (12.5 m/s). This is the most stringent requirement yet applied to helicopters which in the past had been required to be designed to touchdown speeds of only 10 or 12 ft/s (3 or 3.5 m/s). The

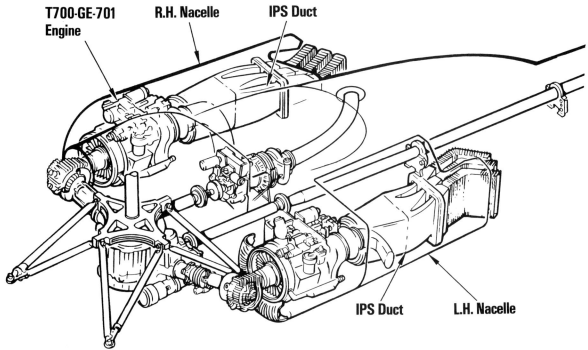

*AH-64 Engine Installation*

first task was to design the landing gear to make it absorb as much energy as possible. The options available to the landing gear designer present a dilemma. On the one hand, he would like to use a retracting landing gear to achieve a higher maximum speed and better fuel efficiency; but on the other hand, he knows that a retracted gear gives him little opportunity to use it as an effective energy-absorbing device in a crash landing. Faced with the 42 ft/s (12.5 m/s) requirement, Hughes Helicopter opted for a non-retractible landing gear. It chose a 'trailing arm' type with the oleo shock absorber in the supporting strut. The shock absorber contains a diaphragm that ruptures during a hard landing. Energy is dissipated at a controlled rate as the trapped hydraulic fluid squirts through a metred orifice. To absorb more energy following the complete collapse of the landing gear, the bottom of the fuselage was made crushable. Finally, the seats were made to 'stroke' or to settle downward while absorbing even more

*Pilot Acceleration during Vertical Crash Landing.*

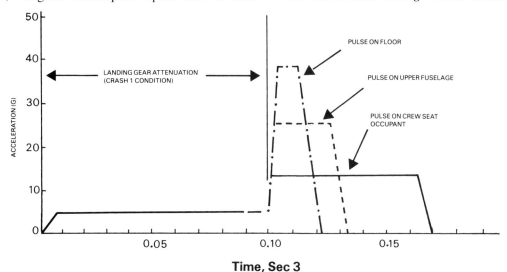

energy. The resulting survivable acceleration at the pilot's seat is shown by the time-history measured during a drop tower test.

Besides limiting the accelerations to survivable levels, good design practice requires that in a crash, the cockpit volume does not decrease by more than 15 per cent and that anything that the head is likely to come in contact with is frangible. The wing and tail surfaces should break away cleanly so as not to place high loads on the structure surrounding the occupants.

The Apache forward fuselage is built with two keel-like structural members serving as skids in case of a crash with forward speed. This prevents the nose from 'plowing in' and also provides space for the turreted gun to be forced up into the lower fuselage without entering either cockpit.

### Fuel Tanks

Fuel tanks in a military helicopter warrant special consideration for both combat damage and for crash damage. They should be self-sealing after being pierced with a round and they should not catch on fire even if the round is incendiary. One approach is to fill the tanks with 'rectulated foam' which acts much like a sponge and isolates the space above the fuel into such small units that a flame cannot progress. The other is to provide an internal tank lining of soft elastic material much like that used on self-sealing automobile tyres and to use a separate system to purge the oxygen out of the tank

*A typical installation for wire cutters is shown on the Bell OH-58D.*

above the fuel. On the AH-64, this is done with 'nitrogen inerting' using a system that removes almost all of the oxygen from air and pumps the resulting nitrogen-rich gas into the tanks above the remaining fuel. Fuel lines are provided with check valves that close if the line is broken. In other cases, designers have chosen to mount the fuel tanks externally and have provided the means by which they will break free of the aircraft in a crash while maintaining their structural integrity to avoid spilling fuel.

## Wire Strike Protection

An enemy projectile is expected to do damage during wartime, but the helicopter is subject to similar damage at any time if it runs into a wire or cable. Because the helicopter finds its greatest usefulness close to the ground, wire strike accidents are all too common. There are two means of decreasing this type of accident. The most obvious is to avoid running into wires in the first place. This means either knowing precisely where they are or being able to detect them and to take evasive action. The first is out of the hands of the designer, but the second is perhaps amenable to a scientific solution in the form of a special radar system that has a fine enough resolution to be able to pinpoint signals being reflected from such a small target as a wire. Several of these systems have been demonstrated in prototype form and may some day be available for production. Another possibility that would apply to wires carrying electrical current is to detect them by means of their own magnetic fields.

The other solution for reducing wire-strike accidents is to let the helicopter run into the wires and then cut them quickly and cleanly with devices having sharp blade leading edges attached above and below the nose and at the landing gear. A typical installation for wire cutters is shown on the Bell OH-58D.

# Ditching

Not all crash landings are on land. Helicopters intended for operation at sea must also be capable of being safely ditched. This means that not only must the structure be strong enough to withstand the impact loads on contact with the water, but the helicopter must float upright and remain water-tight in specified sea states long enough to insure rescue. For the unfortunate cases where the helicopter sinks, provisions must be made for quick emergency egress and for all the equipment that is required for survival at sea.

Emergency exits must be clearly marked with lights and large enough that they can be used by people wearing emersion suits and life preservers. One set of tests resulted in the interesting observation that if the exits appear to be too big, two people would try to go through at the same time with the result that both would become trapped.

# Icing and Deicing

Detecting and removing ice from critical components in flight has been state-of-the-art on airplanes for many years, but until recently, few helicopters outside the Soviet Union had been equipped to do so. There are two reasons for this: the mechanics of deicing a rotor are much more difficult than deicing a wing, and icing conditions in the Temperate Zones are encountered so rarely in normal helicopter operation that it is hard to justify the weight and expense of a system that on any one helicopter may never be needed. With the realisation that future military operations will not be restricted to the Temperate Zones, most of the specifications for military helicopters in the West since about 1970 have included requirements for systems that will allow flight into known icing conditions.

## Icing Conditions

The severity of icing depends both on tempera-ture and on the 'liquid water content' of the air measured in grams of water per cubic metre. In practice, the aeroplane community defines severity by the distance travelled while picking up half an inch of ice on a small probe. If 40 nm (74 km) are required, the icing is 'light'. If only 10 nm (19 km) are needed, then it is 'heavy'. Obviously these criteria do not apply directly to helicopters but they are still embedded in the terminology for icing severity.

Even at below freezing temperatures, it is possible for water droplets in the form of fog, drizzle, or rain to remain in liquid state as long as there is nothing for the first ice crystal to form on, such as a speck of dust. When an aircraft flies by, it provides the required foreign body and the 'super-cooled' droplets will immediately freeze to any surface on which they impinge. It is, of course, the forward-facing surfaces that receive the brunt of the impingement, especially on the very leading edge of a component at the 'stagnation point', where one streamline of air is brought to a complete stop. Small objects are more efficient in picking up ice than are larger ones. The figure shows the results of exposing three cylinders to the same icing conditions.

*Effect of Object Size on Ice Accumulation*

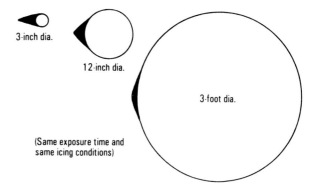

3-inch dia.

12-inch dia.

3-foot dia.

(Same exposure time and same icing conditions)

The reason for the significant difference is that the larger the cylinder, the more warning it projects ahead to distort the approaching flow field and to deflect the oncoming droplets to either side. Thus the smaller a blade leading edge or an engine inlet lip, the more sensitive it will be to icing conditions.

## Rotor Deicing

Ice on the main and tail rotor blades can have potentially bad effects while building up and possibly catastrophic effects when breaking loose. Since the blades are going faster than any other part of the helicopter, they encounter more drops of water per second and, because of their high collection efficiency, accrete ice at a faster rate. On the other hand, compression of the air at the stagnation point at the leading edge of the blade raises the temperature as much as 22°C at the very tip. For this reason, blade tips often remains ice-free while ice builds up on the inboard sections.

Blade ice that is allowed to accumulate will eventually shed because of centrifugal forces, airloads, blade flexing, or flying into warmer air. When it does, it often goes off from one blade at a time. The resultant imbalance can produce severe vibration in the aircraft and high oscillating loads in the main and tail rotor support structures. At the same time, the tail rotor blades may be damaged by ice flung off the main rotor blades or vice-versa.

Before the ice sheds, it degrades the aerodynamic characteristics of the blade airfoil by forming irregular shapes that increase drag and decrease the maximum lift capabilities. The figure shows some of the shapes that have been observed on airfoil leading edges following flight in icing conditions. The shapes apparently vary as a function of the temperature.

*Ice Shapes Observed on Leading Edge*

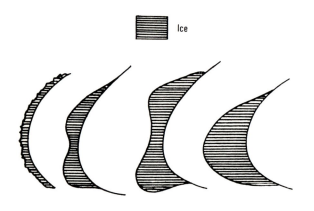

The requirement to increase power to maintain speed or a rate of climb may give the alert pilot the first indication of ice. This might not only be due to the drag penalty of the ice on the blades but also to the additional weight of ice on the helicopter as a whole.

The degraded aerodynamic characteristics will also jeopardise the ability to autorotate in case of an engine flameout that might have also been caused by icing conditions. Ice on the blades has several detrimental effects on the autorotational capability:

1. Because of the increased drag, the power required is greater and thus the autorotative rate of descent must be higher to generate the needed power from the change in potential energy. This gives the pilot less time to try to restart the engine.

2. Because the rate of descent is higher, the collective pitch required to maintain normal rotor speed is lower. If the designers did not foresee this possibility, the collective downstop may be too high to obtain the desired rotor speed. The figure shows the trends as affected by ice.

*Autorotative Rotor Speed Trends*

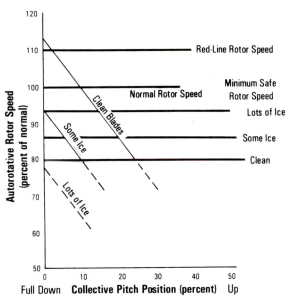

3. Because the maximum lift capability is lower, the minimum safe rotor speed will be higher. With much ice, it may actually be higher than the speed that can be achieved on the collective downstop.

4. Because the drag is higher, the ability to build up rotor speed in a cyclic flare will be lower reducing the energy available for the final touchdown.

5. Because the maximum lift is lower, the load

factor that can be generated by the final collective pull will be lower.

Any one of these effects might be enough to change a routine good weather manoeuvre into a serious winter accident.

## Deicing Systems

It is generally accepted that ice can be allowed to build up to about a quarter of an inch halfway out on today's blades before it becomes dangerous. At that thickness, it should be removed. Most deicing systems for helicopter blades now use electrical heating blankets although some other systems have been tried in the past. These blankets are either installed as external devices on the leading edge of the blades or buried below one layer of leading edge skin. In any case, they should not distort the aerodynamic shape of the airfoil and they should have good erosion resistance to rain and sand. Electricity for them is produced by generators mounted on the transmission or engine and then transmitted to the blades through slip rings at the rotor hub. The blankets are divided into zones and each is periodically heated. This melts the bond between the skin and the ice that has accumulated since the last cycle, allowing centrifugal forces to fling the ice off. Corresponding zones of every blade are heated at the same time to minimise possible imbalance. The interval between heatings of any one blade segment is determined by the icing severity measured with an ice detector, sometimes mounted in an engine inlet to ensure a flow over it even in hover.

By popping the ice off quickly from the leading edge, there will be little water to run back and freeze on the trailing edge. This type of cyclic deicing system takes much less power than would an anti-icing system that would continuously try to keep the whole blade above freezing.

## Looking for a Better System

No one likes the cost or complexity of an electrical deicing system, nor the weight of the over-size electrical generator that must be carried around all the time for the few times that icing conditions exist. There is therefore high motivation for finding other methods of ice protection and a large number have been tried in the past. One is to attempt to break up the ice with blade bending induced by sudden cyclic, collective, or rotor-speed changes. This has seemed to work on some helicopters in special circumstances but not on others. Another approach that has been used on helicopters is an adaption of one once used on aeroplane propellers in which antifreeze fluid is allowed to run out the blades through holes in the surface from a distribution system at the hub. So far, this system has not been adopted for modern helicopters because of the difficulty in obtaining an uniform distribution and because of the dangerous fatigue sensitivity produced by holes in highly loaded skins. Another system that has been recently demonstrated in prototype form is a version of the pneumatic deicing boot long used on aeroplane wings in which periodic deformation of the boot breaks the ice and allows it to be discarded.

A better way than any of these would consist of a paint, paste, or tape that would be 'ice phobic' yet could still stand up to the erosive effects of dust, sand, and rain.

## Engine Protection

Ice can produce two types of problems for turbine engines. If ice accumulations block or change the effective shape of the inlet passages so that the air approaching the compressor is distorted, the resulting non-uniform velocity distributions may lead to compressor stall with a possible engine flame-out. The other problem is that if the ice accumulation breaks off in chunks, they may be large enough to damage the compressor. For these reasons, the helicopter designer has adopted the methods of the aeroplane designer who faces the same problems. One method is to bury electric heating blankets in the skin of the inlet leading edge and other critical areas. An alternative is to use hot engine compressor bleed air to keep the surfaces warm. These systems are classified as anti-ice systems since they prevent the ice from forming at all times as contrasted to the de-ice systems preferred for the main and tail rotor blades that allow the ice to build up and then periodically remove it.

## Windshield Anti-Icing

Besides the rotor blades and the engine, the windshield needs to be kept free of ice so the pilot can see where he is going. This is generally now done electrically with conducting film sandwiched inside the transparency material. Alternate methods use hot engine compressor bleed air with suitable ducting.

# Escape!

Pilots of combat aircraft have had parachutes since after the First World War, to give them a chance to survive if something goes wrong in the air. Pilots of combat helicopters, so far, have not been given that option. There are two reasons for this situation. The first is that the proximity of the rotor makes it very difficult to provide a safe escape route upward and the helicopter is often flying too low to make downward ejection feasible. The other reason is that the helicopter carries its own 'parachute' in the form of its rotor which in most cases of something going wrong can provide for a safe landing through autorotation.

These two reasons do not keep those concerned from trying to develop in-flight escape systems. The Rotor System Research Aircraft (RSRA) of the NASA has been equipped with upward ejection seats that would be used after the rotor blades were jettisoned by explosive charges cutting through each blade root. The Lockheed Cheyenne prototype was equipped with a downward ejection seat for flight test conditions deemed to have an element of danger. Other proposals have included sideward ejection but none of these are incorporated in current helicopters. Upward ejection for the crew will be a flight-test feature of the V-22 Osprey – a relatively easy choice since the rotors are never above the cockpit. Of course, when this aircraft is carrying passengers, it will have to abide by the rule that has always applied: 'Either everybody has a parachute or nobody does.'

The other concern for escape is from a helicopter that has crashed or ditched. As part of his concern about crash worthiness, the designer must guard against the possibility of the crew or passengers being trapped by doors or canopies that cannot be opened after being deformed. The usual solution is to provide explosive devices that can blow a panel off or create a new emergency exit.

# Detail Design

## The Guidelines

To insure a coordinated effort during the design, two documents are prepared that the members of the design team use as guidance. One is the System Specification and the other is the Design Criteria.

### The System Specification

This is the agreement with the customer as to what the helicopter will be in terms of its performance, safety, and operational capabilities. In most cases, its format and content are based on the military customer's original Request For Proposal with modifications made during the contract negotiation. In the case of a commercial programme, the 'customer' may be a marketing or sales organisation representing the needs of the marketplace.

*A Partial Drawing Tree*

## The Design Criteria

This is a companion to the System Specification. It is written by the contractor but approved by the customer and sets forth all of the ground rules for designing the structure. These include the design loads in flight and during ground handling and weapon firing for each component, operating speeds in the rotating parts, envelopes of load factor and sideslip versus speed, design crash conditions, the fatigue loading spectrum, and the extremes of environmental conditions, and all other criteria deemed significant.

## The Drawing Tree

When aircraft were truly experimental machines, designers such as the Wright Brothers or Igor Sikorsky did not have to be particularly fussy about the working drawings that were sent to the shop. As aircraft became more and more complicated, it became necessary to support the shop

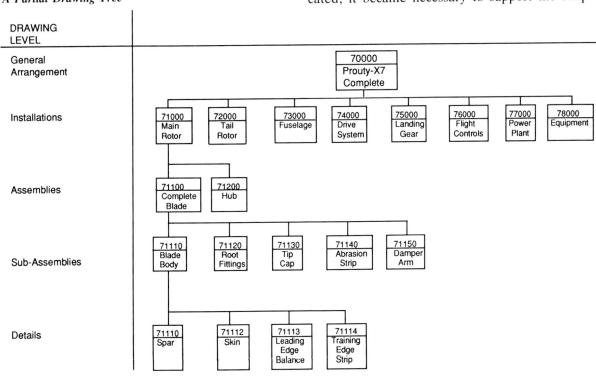

with more detailed and organised drawings to avoid mistakes.

The system evolved into what is called a 'drawing tree' although as drawn, it looks more like a root system. At the top is the General Arrangement Drawing. Down from it at assigned levels are drawings for installations, assemblies, sub-assemblies, and individual details. A logical numbering system allows the user to relate any individual drawing to the complete system. Shown is a partial drawing tree that illustrates the system for some details of the main rotor blade.

Each engineering organisation evolves its own system for the format of the drawings. The following description is considered to be typical.

Each drawing has a title block indicating the aircraft, that is being depicted, the drawing number, and the next drawing up the drawing tree. It also provides spaces for signatures of the designer, the checker, appropriate staff members involved in weight, stress, aerodynamics, producibility, cost, and supervisors designated for various components and levels on the drawing tree. Space for a bill of materials and also space to keep track of subsequent changes are included.

*A Typical Drawing Title Block*

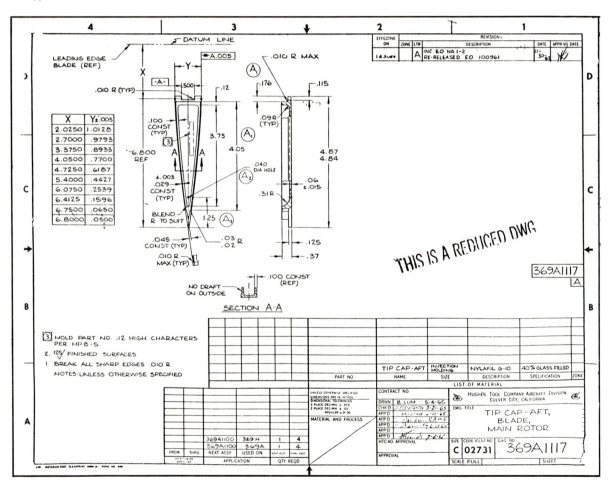

*A Typical Release Engineering Order*

The drawing is sent to the shop along with an Engineering Order (EO), marked 'RELEASE' that essentially says: 'Make this'.

# Changes

Changes are easy to make at the beginning of a project when only a few people are involved, but as the project matures through preliminary design, detail design, prototype construction, and then into production the motivation to avoid making changes becomes stronger and stronger and when changes are unavoidable, they must be fully justified and documented to insure that every person who is involved is informed.

Changes are forced by several different kinds of situations. Some may be requested by the customer in the form of an Engineering Change Proposal (ECP). He uses these if he wants the

aircraft modified to incorporate a newly-developed weapon or to carry equipment for a mission for which the machine had not originally been designed. This can happen even when the aircraft is still in preliminary design although it is more usual after it has been in production for a time. When feasible, these requests are welcomed by the contractor since he knows that the customer intends to pay for them. This may not be the case if the request reflects dissatisfaction with an aircraft that is not meeting contractual guarantees.

Other changes of both major and minor significance may be contractor-initiated. They may also be ECPs based on suggestions for improving the capabilities that the contractor has been studying, but they may also be of less significance such as correcting original design errors involving two solid objects being destined for the same space, errors in processing instructions, or just errors in dimensioning. Other changes may be prompted by the failure of the first structural parts to pass static and fatigue tests in the laboratory or later by the realisation from flight tests that the actual loads are different than had been used for design. Sometimes changes are found desirable to ease the difficulty in manufacturing a part or assembly or to reduce its weight or cost.

Before changes can be made, they must be approved by the appropriate level of authority. During preliminary design this may be done on an informal basis by the Project Engineer or his delegated assistant, but as the project matures, a 'Change Board' is established that includes members of both the design and staff departments to screen the proposed changes. The engineer making the proposal, after convincing his department manager that it is valid, obtains the concurrence of the appropriate staff members if the change involves weight, stress, aerodynamics, or cost and submits the proposal to the Change Board in the form of an Engineering Change Request Recommendation (ECRR). If it

is controversial, he may be called before the board to defend it. The Change Board may approve, reject, or if the change has serious consequences, elect to defer the decision to the 'Senior Change Board' consisting of the Chief Engineer and his Department Managers. (Note: In some tightly-run projects known as 'skunk works' some of these steps may be shortened by authoritative decisions made by the Project Manager).

Approved changes are made through the use of Engineering Orders marked 'CHANGE' that become a permanent part of the drawing file as the original is modified and copies of the Change EO are attached to all issued copies of the drawing.

The Change EO will include the reason for the change and if the helicopter is already in production will designate at which point in the production run the change will become effective.

At some point, it may be decided to start a drawing all over in which case a Cancellation EO will be issued.

## A Typical Change EO

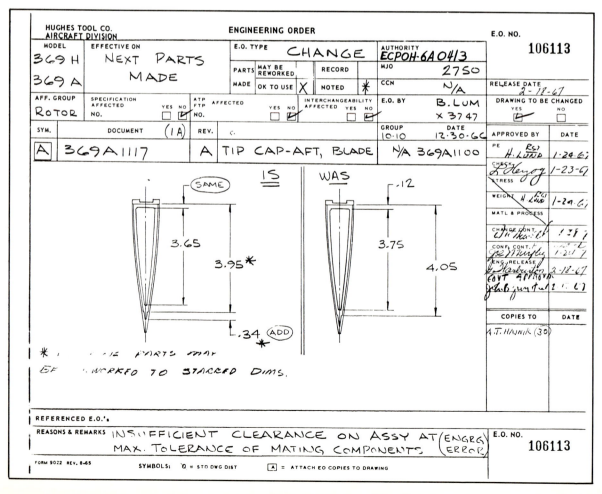

# Selecting Components

The military customer has a lot to say about what it is that will go into the helicopter that he is buying. In almost all cases, he specifies the weapons and the Mission Equipment Package (MEP) associated with communication, navigation, survival, and fire control. In some cases, he even specifies the engine.

| T O Rating (h p ) | Engine | Source | Decade First Devlp. | Drive | Where Used |
|---|---|---|---|---|---|
| 420 | Allison 250-C20B | US | 1960 | Front | BO 105 |
| 420 | Allison T53-A-720 | US | 1960 | Front | OH-58D |
| 444 | PZL GTD-350 | Poland | 1950 | Rear | Mi-2 |
| 500 | Allison 250-C28 | US | 1960 | Front | Bell 206 |
| 591 | Turbomeca Astazou XIVH | France | 1960 | Front | SA 341 |
| 641 | Turbomeca Arriel | France | 1970 | Front | AS 350 |
| 684 | Textron Lycoming LTS 101 750C-1 | US | 1960 | Front | Bell 222 |
| 700 | Allison 250-C30 | US | 1960 | Front | OH-58D |
| 838 | Turbomeca TM 333B | France | 1980 | Front | SA 365 |
| 858 | Turbomeca Astazou XIVM | France | 1960 | Front | SA 342 |
| 895 | Rolls Royce Mk 1004 | UK | 1970 | Front | A 129 |
| 960 | Pratt & Whitney PT6B-36 | Canada | 1960 | Front | S-76B |
| 1132 | RR Gem 60-3/1 Mk 530 | UK | 1970 | Front | Lynx-3 |
| 1200 | Allison/Garret T800 | US | 1980 | Front | LHX |
| 1350 | GE T58-GE-8F | US | 1950 | Rear | SH-2 |
| 1400 | Textron Lycoming T53-L-13 | US | 1960 | Front | UH-1H |
| 1480 | Turbomeca Turmo III C4 | France | 1960 | Rear | SA 321 |
| 1485 | Textron Lycoming T53-L-703 | US | 1960 | Front | AH-1S |
| 1500 | Isotov TV2-117A | USSR | 1970 | Rear | Mi-8 |
| 1500 | GE T58-GE-100 | US | 1950 | Rear | CH-3E |
| 1535 | RR Gnome H14001 | UK | 1950 | Rear | Sea King |
| 1560 | GE T700-700 | US | 1970 | Front | UH-60 |
| 1696 | GE T700-701 | US | 1970 | Front | AH-64 |
| 1800 | Pratt & Whitney PT6T-3 | Canada | 1960 | Front | Bell 212 |
| 1835 | Turbomeca Makila | France | 1970 | Rear | AS 332 |
| 1870 | GE T58-GE-16 | US | 1950 | Rear | CH-46E |
| 2100 | RR/Turbomeca RTM 322 | UK/Fr | 1980 | Front | EH-101 |
| 2225 | Isotov TV3-117V | USSR | 1970 | Rear | Mi-24/Ka-27 |
| 2930 | Textron Lycoming T5508D | US | 1970 | Front | Bell 214 |
| 3750 | Textron Lycoming T55-L-712 | US | 1970 | Front | CH-47D |
| 4075 | Textron Lycoming AL5512 | US | 1970 | Front | Boeing 234 |
| 4380 | GE T64-GE-416 | US | 1960 | Front | CH-53E |
| 6000 | Allison 501 M80C | US | 1950 | Front | V-22 |
| 6500 | Soloviev D-25VF | USSR | 1960 | Rear | Mi-6 |
| 11400 | Lotarev C-136 | USSR | 1970 | Rear | Mi-26 |

# Engine Selection

At any one time, the list of suitable engines is limited. The designer of the military helicopter must consider the country of origin, the state-of-the-art of the technology, and perhaps whether the engine drives from the front or the rear. Out of the following list of turboshaft engines available in 1987, he may find only one or two in the power range that is suitable for his new design.

It may be seen from this list that there are still a great number of available engines that trace their lineage back to the beginning of the turboshaft era. Since by now, these engines have had most of their development problems solved, they are candidates for those programmes for which engine risk is to be minimised. This is apparently why the Bell/Boeing V-22 – which has risks simply associated with its revolutionary tilt rotor configuration – will initially fly with the Allison 501 that was first used on such 1950 era turboprop aeroplanes as the Lockheed Electra. The more recently developed engines can usually boast of a higher power-to-weight ratio and lower specific fuel consumption achieved with higher compression ratios and higher turbine operating temperatures. These improvements have come in an evolutionary manner and will probably continue for some time into the future.

# Weapons

When it comes to weapon selection, the customer usually specifies the makeup of the weapon suite. It will, of course, depend on whether the helicopter is to be used for defensive or aggressive purposes. At the present time, defensive weapons primarily consist of machine guns of 7.62 or 12.7 mm (30 or 50 calibre) to return ground fire – to 'keep their heads down'. Aggressive weapons are more likely to be heavy guns of 20 to 30 mm or missiles either unguided or guided, or even torpedoes.

For many of these systems, the only design decision is how to support them on the structure. For others, the airframe designer has to do some serious thinking about the interface between helicopter and weapon. One of these subjects for thought is whether a gun should be mounted in a turret or rigidly fastened to the airframe as on many fixed-wing aircraft. The fixed gun is lighter, easier to streamline, and is easier to align

with the gun sight. Its disadvantage, however, is that it must be pointed by pointing the entire aircraft. Thus it cannot respond as quickly to suddenly discovered threats as can a gun mounted on a turret that can be quickly brought to bear on a target even while taking evasive action. This is the subject of debate that has no obvious conclusion.

Another gun decision has to be made about where to store ammunition. If the gun is near the nose, and the ammunition is stored adjacent to it, firing the gun will change the aircraft's centre of gravity. On the other hand, storing the ammunition near the centre of gravity makes it necessary to provide long ammunition passages that take up valuable space and may require an inordinately long development time.

Another design decision concerns whether missiles should be carried externally as on the wings of the AH-64 or internally on retracting mechanisms. The external mounting is simpler, lighter, faster to load and unload, but aerodynamically draggier thus requiring more fuel to do the mission.

# Make or Buy?

One of the major decisions that the contractor makes with respect to each aircraft component for which he is responsible is whether to make it or buy it. Some decisions are easy. The aircraft manufacturer probably has neither the capability nor the desire to manufacture hydraulic pumps, actuators, or tyres. Many such items that are suitable for the new helicopter may already be in production, certified airworthy, and can be chosen from vendor's catalogues. In some other cases, special requirements may be such that although the catalogue components are not quite suitable, small changes to them would make them so. Most component manufacturers are eager to make modifications and requalify if they anticipate a substantial production run.

Other components such as the landing gear and the transmission will probably be so unique to the new design that no existing components can be modified. For these, the design, prototype development, and qualification testing will require a brand-new effort. The decision to do the job either partially or wholly 'in-house' will depend on the judgement of capability based on past experience and current workload compared to the same considerations for an outside vendor.

# Building and Testing the Prototype

## The Mock-Up

One of the first uses of the drawings will be to guide the construction of a mock-up. This has three purposes: to check that components really do fit together as the designers meant them to, to give all interested parties a chance to make last minute suggestions for changes, and to supply photographs for the marketing effort. In some programmes, partial mock-ups are built to supplement the overall mock-up. These may concentrate on the cockpit or the power plant-transmission area. Expediency is the key word in selecting material out of which these are constructed. Depending on the urgency and the necessity to achieve accuracy, they can be made of plywood and cardboard or anything up to the actual material of the final product.

Another type of mock-up, called the System Integration Fixture is often built as a more permanent asset. It will contain all of the fuselage structural elements and provide a three-dimensional aid for laying out wiring harnesses, hydraulic lines, and air ducts between the various components.

## Choice of Tooling

Most military projects are done with some sense of urgency so the shop will begin work on actual parts even before the designers have completed their work. (It is said that the engine mounts for the North American P-51 Mustang were being welded on the third day of the project!) One of the decisions that must be made is what kind of tooling – 'soft' or 'hard' – is to be used for the prototype. Soft tooling is quicker to make and less expensive but is not as precise or durable as hard tooling. It is, however, the tooling of choice if it is anticipated that substantial changes will be incorporated in the design before the production phase or if quantity production is uncertain. The choice of hard tooling, with a substantial investment in massive and precise jigs and fixtures, implies a confidence in the design and the desire to achieve a high production rate as soon as possible.

## Testing

### Laboratory Testing

The goal of laboratory testing is to qualify components as being 'air-worthy' as early in the project as is feasible to allow time for redesign if necessary. Structural and mechanical testing will begin as soon as components are available. Structural parts will be subjected to both static and fatigue testing with the loads set forth in the Design Criteria. Depending on the complexity of a part, as many as six specimens may be fatigue tested to establish their fatigue life as affected by 'scatter'. For helicopters intended for marine use, some of these tests may have to be done in the presence of salt spray.

Mechanical components such as gear boxes and actuators will go through endurance and load tests under higher than anticipated loads in order to qualify them. Often these tests will be done under the extremes of temperatures specified in the System Specification.

To insure system compatability, complete systems such as the control system may be assembled on an 'iron bird' where all components can be operated together in a laboratory setting in which troubles can be more conveniently identified and rectified than on the aircraft itself. This is especially helpful for those control systems involving hydraulic systems and stability and control augmentation using sophisticated avionic components.

The testing of the mechanical and avionic parts of the control system may be supplemented by simulator studies. These usually involve programming the equations of motion of the helicopter and the control system into a computer that can run flight instruments or a visual scene to give the test pilots a preview of the flying qualities and the stabilty and control engineers a chance to fine-tune the 'control laws' by adjusting gains and time constants in their avionic systems. Although this sounds quite straight-forward, the experience with this procedure up to this writing has been disappointing; apparently because accurately representing such a complicated device as a helicopter by equations is not yet completely possible.

On a modern military helicopter, the flight control system is not the only one that needs developing. Those systems involving fire control, navigation, and communications, must not only work successfully separately but together as well. Checking for electro-magnetic interference (EMI) is one of the tasks done first in the systems laboratory and then in flight test.

*An Iron Bird test set-up.*

## Rotor Testing

The first completed main and tail rotor assemblies will be tested on whirl towers at rotational speeds well above those expected in flight to verify their structural integrity and the absence of mechanical or aeroelastic instabilities. In some projects, the whirl tower testing may be supplemented by wind tunnel testing either of full scale rotors or of aerodynamically and dynamically similar models.

## The Ground Test Vehicle

Finally, all of the structural and mechanical components will be assembled into the Ground Test Vehicle (GTV) for endurance testing through all of the conditions that can be simulated in a tied-down situation. Only after a period of many hours as specified in the Ground Test Plan will the prototype be cleared for its first flight.

## Flight Test

Before actually taking to the air, the prototype must be put through a series of tests on the ground. The most critical is to demonstrate the absence of ground resonance or any other type

*A Rotor Whirl Tower.*

*The YAH-64 Ground Test Vehicle.*

of mechanical instability that might not have revealed itself during the previous tests. For helicopters equipped with wheels, some taxiing tests may be appropriate.

Finally comes the most significant milestone in the project – the first flight. Depending on the test pilot's initial reaction, the flight may be just a few seconds or considerably longer. The extent of this and subsequent flights will be limited by the 'Flight Release' signed by the procuring or regulatory agency. The pilot's initial objectives are to uncover any adverse characteristics and to begin to open the 'flight envelope' in terms of speed – in all directions – and load factor. He will also attempt to evaluate the chances of making an emergency landing in case of the failure of an engine or other critical component. Following the first flight, the aircraft will be thoroughly inspected while the pilot makes an encouraging report for the benefit of the press and a detailed list of deficiencies for the design team.

The Flight Release will be continually rewritten to allow the flight envelope to be expanded in small increments. One prototype will be designated as the structural aircraft. It will be completely instrumented and its primary duty

will be to lead in opening up the flight envelope while measuring structural loads to compare with those originally used for design and for laboratory testing. If they are significantly different, parts will be redesigned or retested.

While the structural flight envelope is being expanded, data on performance, flying qualities, and the operation of the various systems will be gathered to compare with the guarantees that were written into the System Specification when hopes were high.

In addition to opening up the flight envelope, special flight tests will be done involving possible failures such as of the engine, the hydraulic system, the SCAS, and any other flight-critical system.

Only after the contractor's pilots have opened up the flight envelope and demonstrated the ability to cope with system failures will the test pilots of the procuring agency be allowed to fly. They will do this at several stages during the development and their reports will guide the subsequent adjustments to the design and negotiations between the customer and the contractor prior to entering production.

On a military helicopter programme, the airframe may be only a small part of the system. Subsequent tests of systems involving weapon management, navigation, communication, and other special functions must be completed satisfactorily before the job is done.

# Current Projects

Current military helicopter programmes continue to dominate the international helicopter industry and to be an important, growing part of the world aerospace industry. Besides the eight major manufacturers in the United States and Europe, several nations are developing helicopter technology expertise, often in joint ventures. Australia, Brazil, Canada, China, Indonesia, India and Japan are becoming increasingly important as licensees and will eventually develop their own helicopter industries.

## FRANCE

Prior to rationalisation of the aerospace industry in France there were several individual helicopter manufacturers. These have now been consolidated into one, state-owned conglomerate, Aerospatiale. In 1988, this company was the largest helicopter exporter in the world and the primary civil helicopter supplier in the USA and Japan.

### Aerospatiale

The company offers a range of four basic helicopter designs, covering the major market sectors with the exception of the ultra-light and heavy weight classifications.

Super Puma: this is a medium transport, support and naval helicopter built originally to satisfy a demand from the offshore oil industry.

It is based on the earlier SA 330 Puma design which first flew in 1965 but the Super Puma, with the improved Turbomeca Makila turboshaft engines did not complete its maiden flight until 1978.

AS 332B1 is the basic military tactical support variant with cabin space for up to 21 troops and two aircrew.

AS 332F1 is the naval version, recently sold to Chile, with a folding tail rotor pylon and deck landing assistance device. It is suitable for SAR, anti-ship and anti-submarine warfare.

AS 332M1 is the stretched version of the B1 with seats for 25 troops or six stretchers/11 seated casualties and a standard aircrew of two. It can be recognised by the extra 'portrait' window forward of the cabin door. Recent customers include the Swedish Air Force and Brazilian Navy.

Super Puma Mk2 is the designation of a new version, which first flew in 1987, and was not selected for the Canadian New Shipborne Aircraft competition in 1988. It will continue to be developed.

Gazelle: this light utility helicopter is a part of the Anglo–French Helicopter Agreement of 1967 and initial variants were built under a joint agreement with Westland. The prototype first flew on 7 April 1967 and a production line

*Aerospatiale AS 332F1 Super Puma, with Exocet.*

*Aerospatiale SA 342M Gazelle with HOT.*

continues in Yugoslavia and one was recently closed in Egypt.

SA 342L1 is the current military version, recently delivered to China and powered by the Turbomeca Astazou XIVM turboshaft engine. The normal complement is two aircrew and up to three passengers, but the primary role is anti-tank with the Euromissle HOT wire-guided weapon and the Viviane day/night sight.

SA 342M is the French Army Aviation (ALAT) version of the Gazelle for anti-tank, reconnaissance and armed escort roles.

Ecureuil/Ecureuil 2: the family of light/intermediate helicopters designed for the commercial and corporate markets but now finding a place in Aerospatiale's military strategy. The first Ecureuil flew in 1974 and the type has the English language name of Squirrel and Twin Squirrel, the US marketing name of AStar and TwinStar.

AS 350L1 is the armed reconnaissance version which can be equipped with cannon and rocket pods; the Danish Ministry of Defence ordered the helicopter with SAAB/Emerson Electric HeliTOW anti-tank missiles in 1987.

AS 335M2 is the twin-engined military version for the French Air Force, capable of carrying the MATRA Mistral air-to-air guided weapon. An anti-tank version is being supplied to Brazil.

Dauphin/Panther: the family of twin-engined intermediate helicopters have been a notable export success, including the largest Emergency Medical Service sales in the USA in 1988. The helicopter has not been so successful in the military role however. The first flight was in 1972.

SA 365F is the designation of a naval version, originally developed with Saudi Arabian funding to provide an anti-ship helicopter armed with the Aerospatiale AS 15TT missile. Subsequent sales have included the French (SAR) and Chilean Navies.

AS 365M is the designation of the TM333-engined Panther multi-role, combat support helicopter which first flew in 1986. No orders have been reported for this version even though it is offered with anti-tank and anti-helicopter armament suites.

SA 365N1 is the standard commercial/corporate/EMS version which has been marketed for utility and tactical support roles.

SA 366G1 is the manufacturer's designation for the HH-65A Dolphin now in service with the US Coast Guard; the Israeli Defence Force operates the basic SA 366G version.

## WEST GERMANY

### MBB

The combination of the Messerschmitt, Bolkow and Blohm design houses has produced some original work in rotorhead and other dynamic systems. MBB is a partner with Aerospatiale in Euromissile which includes the HOT helicopter-mounted anti-tank missile in its product range. The company specialises in light twin-engined helicopters and international collaborative programmes.

BO 105CB is the standard production version, sold to the Swedish Army for the anti-tank role. It is in competition with the Gazelle for the standard anti-tank helicopter of the West German Army Aviation (Heeresfliegertruppen) and the Spanish Army Aviation (FAMET) where is was assembled by CASA. It first flew in 1967.

BO 105CBS is the stretched version with a lengthened fuselage and a potential for SAR operations; the Swedish Air Force has ordered four.

BO 105LS is the uprated engine version being produced in Canada.

*Aerospatiale SA 365M Panther (above).*

*MBB BO 105P (PAH-1) (below).*

NBO 105 is the Indonesia licence version, of which more than 110 have been completed at Bandung.

## INTERNATIONAL

Modern helicopter development programmes are expensive and are hard to justify unless the production run is expected to result in many aircraft. Thus it is attractive to combine both the requirements and the resources of two or more nations when starting a new helicopter design.

### E H Industries

The combination of Agusta (Italy) and Westland (UK) to produce a three-engined helicopter. The naval version for the UK Royal Navy and Italian Navy will replace the Sea King helicopter in the anti-submarine role. EH 101's ASW version can also be operated from frigate and destroyer size warships and is being actively considered by Canada and its NSA programme.

The utility version for offshore oil support is also being developed and there are plans for a tactical support variant for battlefield support and other tactical operations. It first flew in 1987.

### Eurocopter

This is the Franco–German (Aerospatiale and MBB) consortium developing the Common Anti-Tank Helicopter (CATH) for the West German Heeresfliegertruppen (designated PAH-2) and the French ALAT (designated HAC-3G). There is also a French ALAT armed escort/protection version known as HAP armed with cannon and air-to-air missiles. Planned first flight is 1992.

### Joint European Helicopters

A four-nation study into the future light attack helicopter for the European nations. Italy (Agusta) and the United Kingdom (Westland) are leading CASA (Spain) and Fokker (Netherlands) in a design study based on the A129 Mangusta, and called Tonal.

### MBB/Kawasaki

The BK 117 is the result of development by MBB (West Germany) and Kawasaki (Japan) to build a twin-engined multi-purpose helicopter for seven passengers and two aircrew. The high tail rotor configuration has made the design attractive to Emergency Medical Service operators. The A-3M version was displayed at the 1985 Paris Air Show but has received no military orders, although trials have been carried out in West Germany.

### MBB/HAL

The West German manufacturer is supporting the Indian aerospace company, HAL, in its bid

*Agusta-Westland EH-101 first pre-production aircraft.*

*Eurocopter PAH-2 engineering mock-up.*

to develop an advanced light helicopter for Indian military needs. The helicopter should fly before the end of 1989.

### MBB/IPTN

The West German manufacturer has signed a development agreement with IPTN (Indonesia) to study a four-seat light helicopter, known as BN 109.

### NH 90

This is the four-nation programme to develop a multi-purpose medium helicopter for the 1990s. The partners are Aerospatiale (France), MBB (West Germany), Agusta (Italy) and Fokker (Netherlands). There are two versions proposed: TTH 90 is the tactical transport helicopter for the future battlefield and NFH 90 is the naval helicopter for small ship operations.

## ITALY

### Agusta

Italy has built several US designs under licence but in the late 1960s commenced their own design programmes, albeit with additional US aid.

A 109A is the twin-engined light helicopter designed for a corporate helicopter market but which has found success as a light attack helicopter in Argentina. The helicopter is also flown by the UK Army Air Corps. It can carry up to six passengers and an aircrew of two pilots.

A 109K is the re-engined version which is being marketed for the anti-tank role and won the Belgian Army's Airmobility 1 competion in late 1988. It is designated a multi-role hot-and-high helicopter by its manufacturer.

A 129 Mangusta (Mongoose) is a two-seat, tandem-place light attack helicopter for the Italian Army Aviation (ALE). It can carry a range of cannon, rockets and anti-tank missiles. A naval version has been proposed and a developed light tactical support version is being considered.

AB 412 Griffon is a development of the Bell 412 helicopter which has been sold to a small number of African nations.

*Agusta A129A Mangusta.*

*Kamov Ka-27 'Helix'.*

AB 412ASW is the developed naval version which remains in production for the Italian MMI and foreign customers.

## USSR

The Soviet Union has two helicopter design bureaux carrying on the work of the early pioneers, Kamov and Mil. Each produces both civil and military helicopters. The Kamov team designs coaxial helicopters and the Mil team, single rotor/tail rotor machines.

### Kamov

Ka-27/28/32 (NATO codename 'Helix') is a twin-engined, naval helicopter which has been operational since 1982. It is a compact aircraft well suited for operations in warships as small as frigates. The civilian version, which has appeared at a large number of Western air shows in the last six years, also holds a number of helicopter performance records.

So far only identified by its NATO codename 'Hokum', a new high performance battlefield helicopter with a reportedly specialist anti-helicopter role. Jane's Defence Weekly reported in August 1988 that the helicopter's development had been delayed by problems with the flight control system.

Mil Mi-14/17 (NATO codenames 'Haze' and 'Hip H' respectively) represent a continued upgrade of the original Mi-8 utility and battlefield support helicopter, the prototype of which originally flew in public in 1961. Since then, the US Department of Defense estimates that more that 10 000 have been built both for civil and military uses. The Mi-17 are used as medium transports carrying up to 32 passengers and the heavily modified as a shore-based anti-submarine and mine countermeasures aircraft.

The Mi-24 (NATO codename 'Hind') is the primary Soviet assault and attack helicopter which since its first flight in 1972 has been widely exported. In addition to its crew of two (or three in some versions), it has provisions for carrying up to eight combat-equipped troops.

Mi-26 (NATO codename 'Halo') is the world's largest operational helicopter with a maximum gross weight of 123 450 lb (56 000 kg). It is used as a heavy transport both in Soviet civil and military operations, particulary in Siberia.

*Mil Mi-17 'Hip-H' (back) and Mil Mi-8 'Hip-C' (foreground).*

*Mil Mi-24 'Hind D'.*

Mi-28 (NATO codename 'Havoc') is latest Soviet battlefield helicopter design and is scheduled to enter operational service with Group of Soviet Forces Germany in 1992. It has a tandem seat arrangement strongly reminicent of the AH-64A Apache.

## UNITED KINGDOM

### Westland

The sole British helicopter producer is now partly owned by United Technologies, the parent of Sikorsky Aircraft. Westland and Sikorsky have been involved in helicopter licencing for more than 40 years.

Super Lynx is the family name of the latest versions of the Army Lynx and Naval Lynx helicopters which are in quantity service with the UN, NATO and friendly armed forces.

Battlefield Lynx is the commercial name of the British Army's Lynx AH Mk9 light battlefield utility helicopter for the airmobile role, carrying 10 troops. The first Lynx flew in 1971.

Advanced Sea King is the latest development of the Sikorsky S-61/SH-3 design. It has been ordered by the Indian Navy for anti-submarine and anti-ship warfare, as well as for naval utility duties. A number of Sea Kings with airborne early radar radomes were modified as a result of the South Atlantic conflict. It entered operational service with the UK Royal Navy in 1969.

The WS-70A Black Hawk is the armed version of the S-70 Black Hawk.

## UNITED STATES OF AMERICA

The world's largest single market for military and civil helicopters with the US Army's

*Mi-26 'Halo'.*

*Westland Army Lynx.*

inventory standing at over 8000 helicopters in 1988. There remain five manufacturers of military helicopters: Bell, Boeing, Kaman, McDonnell Douglas, and Sikorsky.

They have been fiercely independent in the past, but with the increased costs of high technology programmes, like the US Army's LHX (Light Helicopter Experiment) and the V-22 tilt-rotor, they have formed teams. Bell/Boeing have developed the V-22 Osprey; Bell/McDonnell Douglas have formed the Super-Team to develop an LHX option which is competition for the Boeing/Sikorsky FirstTeam.

## Bell Helicopter Textron

Model 205 series is the well-known UH-1 Huey/Iroquois utility helicopter in several versions. Since the original prototype, the YH-40, flew in 1956 it has approximately doubled in gross weight and in installed power. The 204/205 series are powered by a single Lycoming Textron T-53 engine; remains in production in Turkey to satisfy local defence needs.

Model 212/412 series is a development of the 205, bringing twin-engined safety with the Pratt & Whitney Canada PT-6 TwinPac, especially for overwater operations. The 212 is tandem-bladed and the 412 (latest model is the 412SP in service with Norway) is four-bladed. Production is centred in Canada, with Agusta having an important licence agreement. The 412 is credited with carrying 12 passengers and two aircrew.

Model 209 series is the single-engined AH-1F/S Cobra tandem-seat attack helicopter for the US, Greek and Thai armies and the AH-1W Super-Cobra for the US Marine Corps. The latter is powered by two General Electric T700 engines. The Cobra uses the same dynamic systems as the UH-1.

The Model 206/406 series is based on the

*Westland Commando.*

*The Bell UH-1D.*

*Bell OH-58D Aeroscout.*

highly successful JetRanger/LongRanger series of civilian helicopters. The OH-58C Kiowa is the standard US Army utility/reconnaissance helicopter and this light helicopter is used as a trainer. The OH-58D is a rebuild of the OH-58 with the world's first operational mast-mounted sight above the main rotor hub. It is in service with the US Army; the export version is the 406 Combat Scout which has been ordered by Saudi Arabia.

### Bell/Boeing

The V-22 Osprey is a tilt-rotor aircraft being developed as a medium weight, high speed transport for the US Marine Corps. It was rolled out in May 1988 and should fly in 1989.

### Boeing

The CH-47D Chinook is the completely rebuilt medium transport for the US Army. The export version is in service with the UK Royal Air Force and several other large operators.

### Kaman

The Seasprite is being produced in the standard US Navy ASW version and was originally

*Bell AH-1S Modernised Cobra.*

*Bell-Boeing V-22 Osprey.*

procured by the US Navy during 1960-1970 and then went out of production. In 1981, production was resumed to allow some of the smaller warships that could not handle the larger Sikorsky SH-60B Seahawk which was about to enter service. It has a crew of four.

## McDonnell Douglas

Model 500MD Defender is the basic version of the light helicopter formerly designed by Hughes Helicopters. It remains in production in South Korea (for the US market) and Japan. The more advanced 530MG Defender has a small but steady market for special operations.

Apache is the world's most advanced opera-

*Boeing Chinook HC Mk1.*

*Kaman 5H-2F.*

tional attack helicopter which first flew in 1975 and serves the US Army as its Advanced Attack Helicopter (AAH). It is capable of a full day/night/adverse weather anti-armour role and has recently added an anti-helicopter capability to its mission equipment package.

### Sikorsky

Super Stallion is the West's largest helicopter with a maximum take off weight of 73 500 lb (33 340 kg) with external payload. The current versions are the CH-53E Super Stallion for the US Navy and US Marine Corps, the MH-53E Sea Dragon for the US Navy and the S-80M Sea Dragon for the Japanese Maritime Self-Defence

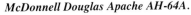

*McDonnell Douglas Apache AH-64A.*

*Sikorsky CH-53E Super Stallion.*

Force. The Super Stallion has three engines although earlier marks (known as the Sea Stallion) had but two.

Black Hawk is the battlefield helicopter version of the S-70 design and includes the UH-60A of which more than 1000 have been delivered to the US Army as its standard medium utility helicopter. The helicopter has recently been ordered by Turkey. Export versions of the Black Hawk are designated S-70A, including the Australian Army's S-70A-9 version.

EH-60A is the US Army special electronic missions aircraft, known as Quick Fix and the MH-60 versions are for special operations.

S-70C Black Hawk, based on a commercial version, is in service with the Taiwanese Air Force for SAR and special operations.

The naval version of the S-70 is called the Seahawk and has a different undercarriage arrangement to the battlefield version to suit decklanding. The standard version is the SH-60B Seahawk, the air vehicle for the LAMPS III programme. Other variants are:

*Sikorsky UH-60A Black Hawk.*

SH-60F Oceanhawk is the US Navy Sea King replacement for the inner zone ASW from aircraft carriers.

S-70B-2 Seahawk is the Royal Australian Navy version for the FFG-7 class frigates; Spain is also receiving the export S-70B. SH-60J Seahawk will be built by Mitsubishi, under licence.

The S-76 civil helicopter design has been modified by Sikorsky for a battlefield role and is proposed for a naval anti-ship role. The Philippines Air Force operates the AUH-76 version but the company is now offering the H-76B Eagle (with the Pratt & Whitney Canada PT-6 TwinPac) as a multi-role battlefield helicopter.

# Helicopter Specification Table

| Aircraft | Manufacturer | Model | No. Engines | Take Off Rating, one engine (hp) | Vne (knots) | Cruise Speed (knots) | Max Climb (ft/min) | Service Ceiling (ft) | Hover Ceiling IGE | Hover Ceiling OGE | Range, Std Tanks (Naut Miles) | Range, Aux Tanks (Naut Miles) | Empty | Max. Payload | Usable Fuel (Std Tanks) | Normal T O | Max. T O | Main Rotor Dia (ft) | Tail Rotor Dia | Length of Fuse | Width | Height (overall) | Cabin Length (internal) | Cabin Width | Cabin Height | Max Seating |
|---|---|---|---|---|---|---|---|---|---|---|---|---|---|---|---|---|---|---|---|---|---|---|---|---|---|---|
| *FRANCE* | | | | | | | | | | | | | | | | | | | | | | | | | | |
| AS 332B1 Super Puma | Turbomeca | Makila 1A1 | 2 | 1835 | 150 | 150 | 1397 | 13450 | 8850 | 5250 | 334 | — | 94500 | — | 2678 | — | 19841 | 51.2 | 10.0 | 51.0 | 12.4 | 16.1 | 19.9 | 5.9 | 5.1 | 25 |
| SA 342L1 Gazelle | Turbomeca | Astazou XIVM | 1 | 858 | 151 | 140 | 1537 | 13450 | 9975 | 7715 | 383 | — | 2184 | — | 936 | — | 4410 | 34.4 | 2.3 | 39.3 | 6.7 | 10.5 | 7.2 | 4.3 | 4.0 | 5 |
| SA 365M Panther | Turbomeca | TM 333 B | 2 | 838 | 160 | 150 | 1575 | — | 10500 | 8200 | 400 | — | 5992 | — | 1957 | — | 8928 | 39.1 | 3.0 | 37.5 | 10.5 | 13.2 | 7.5 | 6.7 | 4.6 | 10–14 |
| *GERMANY (WEST)* | | | | | | | | | | | | | | | | | | | | | | | | | | |
| MBB BO 105CB | Allison | 250-C20B | 2 | 420 | 145 | 131 | 1575 | 17000 | 8400 | 5300 | 310 | 540 | 2813 | 5999 | 1005 | 5291 | 5511 | 32.3 | 6.2 | 28.1 | 8.3 | 9.8 | 6.1 | 3.9 | 1.9 | 5 |
| *INTERNATIONAL* | | | | | | | | | | | | | | | | | | | | | | | | | | |
| EH 101 | RR/Turbo | RTM322 | 3 | 2100 | 174 | 150 | — | — | — | — | 250 | 1000 | 15862 | — | 7599 | 20448 | 28660 | 61.0 | 13.2 | 52.0 | 18.0 | 21.3 | 21.3 | 8.2 | 6.0 | 30 |
| Eurocopter HAP/CATH | MTU/Turbo | MTM 385-R | 2 | 1200–1475 | — | 151 | 1970 | — | — | 3280 | — | — | — | — | — | 11464 | 11905 | 42.7 | 8.9 | — | — | — | — | — | — | 2 |
| *ITALY* | | | | | | | | | | | | | | | | | | | | | | | | | | |
| A 129 Mangusta | Rolls Royce | Gem 2 Mk 1004D | 2 | 895 | 170 | 140 | 2090 | — | 10800 | 7850 | — | — | 5575 | — | 1653 | — | 9039 | 39.0 | 7.3 | 40.3 | 3.1 | 10.9 | — | — | — | 2 |
| *USSR* | | | | | | | | | | | | | | | | | | | | | | | | | | |
| Ka-27/32 'Helix' | Isotov | TV3-117V | 2 | 2225 | 135 | 124 | — | 19685 | — | 4700 | 432 | 513 | — | 11023 | — | 24250 | 27775 | 45.9 | — | 44.3 | — | — | — | — | — | 18 |
| Mi-17 'Hip H' | Isotov | TV3-117V | 2 | 2225 | 135 | 129 | — | 16400 | — | 5775 | 267 | — | 15653 | 6614 | — | 24470 | 28660 | 69.9 | 12.8 | 59.6 | 8.2 | 18.5 | 20.1 | 7.7 | 5.9 | 30–34 |
| Mi-24 'Hind D' | Isotov | TV3-117V | 2 | 2225 | 167 | 159 | 2960 | 14750 | — | 7200 | 105 | — | 18520 | 3300 | — | 24250 | — | 55.8 | 12.8 | 57.4 | — | 21.3 | — | — | — | 2–10 |
| Mi-26 'Halo' | Lotarev | C-136 | 2 | 11400 | 159 | 137 | — | 15100 | 6500 | 3900 | 132 | — | 62170 | 44090 | — | 109125 | 123450 | 105.0 | 24.9 | 110.7 | 26.7 | 26.7 | 39.4 | 10.7 | 10.0 | 93 |
| *UNITED KINGDOM* | | | | | | | | | | | | | | | | | | | | | | | | | | |
| Westland Sea King | Rolls Royce | Gnome H1900IT | 2 | 1465 | 122 | 110 | 2030 | — | 6500 | 4700 | 800 | 940 | 12194 | — | 6318 | 13799 | 21500 | 62.0 | 10.3 | 55.8 | 16.3 | 16.8 | 19.2 | 6.5 | 6.3 | 4–32 |
| Westland Lynx-3 | Rolls Royce | Gem 60-3/1 | 2 | 1132 | — | 140 | 2480 | 6500 | — | 10600 | 340 | 724 | 5683 | — | 1616 | — | 10000 | 42.0 | 7.2 | 43.2 | 9.6 | 12.0 | 6.7 | 5.8 | 4.7 | 2–11 |
| *UNITED STATES* | | | | | | | | | | | | | | | | | | | | | | | | | | |
| Bell UH-1H | AVCO | T53-L-13 | 1 | 1400 | 110 | 110 | 1600 | 12600 | 13600 | 4000 | 276 | — | 5210 | — | 1450 | — | 9500 | 48.0 | 8.5 | 41.9 | 9.7 | 14.5 | — | 7.7 | 4.1 | 2–15 |
| Bell AH-1S | AVCO | T53-L-705 | 1 | 1485 | 170 | 123 | 1620 | 12200 | 12200 | — | 274 | — | 6398 | — | 1684 | 9975 | 10000 | 44.0 | 8.5 | 44.6 | 3.2 | 13.5 | — | — | — | 5 |
| Bell OH-58C | Allison | T63-A-720 | 1 | 420 | 120 | 102 | 1780 | 18900 | 13600 | 8800 | 259 | — | 1464 | — | 475 | — | 3000 | 33.3 | 5.4 | 31.2 | 6.4 | 9.5 | 7.0 | 4.2 | 4.3 | 4 |
| Bell OH-58D | Allison | 250-C30R | 1 | 700 | 130 | 120 | 1540 | 12000 | 12000 | 11200 | 300 | — | 2825 | — | 707 | 4500 | 4500 | 35.0 | 5.4 | 33.8 | 6.5 | 12.7 | — | — | — | 4 |
| Bell/Boeing V-22 | Allison | 501 M80C | 2 | 6000 | 340 | 340 | — | — | — | — | — | 1111 | — | 20700 | 6695 | 33000 | 47500 | 38.0 | — | 57.2 | 15.2 | 20.2 | 24.0 | 6.0 | 6.0 | 2–26 |
| Boeing CH-47D | AVCO | T55-L-712 | 2 | 3750 | 157 | 130 | 1333 | 22500 | — | 5600 | — | — | 22452 | — | 1300 | — | 50000 | 60.0 | — | 51.0 | 12.5 | 18.7 | 30.2 | 7.5 | 6.5 | 35–46 |
| Kaman SH-2F | Gen. Elec. | T58-GE-8F | 2 | 1350 | — | 120 | 2440 | 18600 | — | 5400 | 375 | — | 7040 | — | — | — | 13500 | 44.0 | 8.0 | 40.5 | 12.2 | 15.5 | — | — | — | 3–6 |
| McDonnell Douglas AH-64A | Gen. Elec. | T700-701 | 2 | 1696 | 197 | 160 | — | 21000 | 15000 | 11500 | 260 | 918 | 10760 | — | 2550 | 14445 | 21000 | 48.0 | 9.2 | — | — | 15.3 | — | — | — | 2 |
| Sikorsky CH-53E | Gen. Elec. | T64-GE-416 | 3 | 4380 | — | — | — | 18500 | 11550 | 9500 | 1120 | — | 33226 | 32000 | 6611 | — | 73500 | 79.0 | 20.0 | 73.3 | 8.9 | 28.5 | 30.0 | 7.5 | 6.5 | 58 |
| Sikorsky UH-60A | Gen. Elec. | T700-700 | 2 | 1560 | — | 145 | — | 19000 | 9500 | 5600 | 324 | 880 | 10624 | — | 2327 | 16260 | 20413 | 53.7 | 11.0 | 50.0 | 7.7 | 16.9 | — | — | — | 13–16 |

# The Difficulty of Looking into the Future

The development of any engineering discipline has historically been based on gradual evolution with periods of unexpected revolution. In the helicopter field, the revolutionary developments were the invention of the fully articulated rotor hub in the 1920s, (for the autogiro, not the helicopter); the introduction of the turboshaft engine in the 1950s; the impact of the computer in the 1960s; and the acceptance of composites for rotor blades in the 1970s and for major structural parts in the 1980s. None of these startling revolutionary steps could have been predicted twenty years before and so any present attempt to predict that far into the future must be done with the realisation that yet another revolutionary development may be completely missed in the cloudy crystal ball.

It is not only technical changes that might obscure our vision, but economic, political, environmental, and sociological pressures as well. The post-war prediction that everyone would soon have a ram-jet powered helicopter in his garage was nullified not by the lack of appropriate technology but by those other pressures.

As a student during that same exciting post-war period I recall an incident that happened at the University of Washington in Seattle. McDonnell Aircraft, in their first endeavour with helicopters had brought a rotor model to test in the university wind tunnel. While there, the rotor's designer, Dr Kurt Hohenemser, was asked to address a seminar of aeronautical engineering students. At the end of the presentation, one student asked, 'Do you really think that helicopters will ever be practical'. Dr Hohenemser looked at him directly and said, "Young man, I am an engineer, not a prophet". The helicopter has, of course, become 'practical' but his words still are worth remembering by any engineer who attempts to delve into the future.

One way to illustrate the pitfalls is to go back to some former period and look at the situation then as it related to the next few years. For instance, in 1972, the year that Igor Sikorsky died, the rotary wing projects being talked about with enthusiasm included some that became successful and others that are still waiting. For example:

— Both Sikorsky and Boeing Vertol were selected to build UTTAS prototypes.
— Lockheed was still hopeful that their 220 knots Cheyenne compound attack helicopter would be put into production.
— The MBB BO 105 and the Aerospatiale Gazelle were coming into production.
— Hughes demonstrated a very quiet helicopter.
— The Sikorsky advancing blade concept (ABC) high speed-helicopter was an active and promising project.
— Mil began delivering the Mi-24 'Hind' to the Soviet Armed Forces.
— Almost all airborne avionic equipment and many engineering computers were based on analogue technology.
— The Boeing Vertol heavy lift helicopter was an active and promising project.
— Bell was pursuing the tilt-rotor concept.
— The giant twin-rotor Mi-V-12 was displayed at the Paris Air Show.

In technology, new airfoils were being developed for helicopters after a long quiet spell. A new type of rotor – the circulation control rotor – was going through its initial wind tunnel testing, and composite materials were beginning to show their potential. Microwave landing systems were demonstrated and proclaimed ready for wide-spread usage.

It is evident that anyone attempting to predict the post-1972 future of helicopters based on these clues would have achieved only a fair degree of success.

# What We Can Predict

The primary usefulness of the helicopter either in military or civil roles is its ability to hover and to operate from unprepared sites. For flying between block-long concrete strips such as are envisioned for city-centre to city-centre operations, helicopters would be hard pressed to compete with more efficient STOL aeroplanes. Operators of military and civil emergency vehicles will seldom have the luxury of such facilities so here the helicopter will have no real competition.

Although it is impossible to predict the next revolutionary steps with assurance, the evolutionary steps will primarily be in response to the needs of the present-day military machines. These can be categorised as improvements desired in several fields:

| | |
|---|---|
| **Performance:** | — higher hover figure of merit |
| | — better cruise efficiency |
| | — higher maximum speed |
| **Manoeuvreability:** | — higher load factor |
| | — higher linear and rotational accelerations |
| | — higher linear and rotational velocities |
| **Flying Qualities (better man-machine matching):** | — crisper control with minimum overshoots |
| | — minimum cross-coupling |
| | — minimum gust response |
| | — better hands-off stability |
| **Productivity:** | — lighter and less costly structural, mechanical and electronic components |
| **Safety:** | — better field of view greater crashworthiness greater invulnerability to combat damage |
| | — greater reliability of structural, mechanical, and electronic components |
| **Stealth:** | — minimum signature from visual, aural, radar, infra-red, and electromagnetic radiation standpoints |
| **Availability:** | — improved reliability and maintainability |
| | — quicker repair of combat damage |
| **Comfort:** | — reduced vibration and interior noise |
| | — more comfortable seats |
| | — better control of temperature |

Who knows? Perhaps some of these needs will be met by revolutionary developments.

# INDEX